Waking the Dead:

The Haunting of Natalie Bradford, Part II

L. Sydney Fisher

Legacy Books Unlimited

Books by <u>*L.* Sydney Fisher</u>

STANDALONES
See No Evil
The Devil's Board

The Phoenix Series
The Phoenix Mission, Part I
The Phoenix Codes, Part II

The Bradford Series
The Haunting of Natalie Bradford, Part I
The Haunting of Natalie Bradford, Part II:
Waking the Dead
The Haunted Prophecy of Natalie Bradford:
The Complete Bradford Series

The Haunted Series
Volume I, The Devil's Den
Volume II, The Wilderness
Volume III, Possum Town
Volume IV, On The Haunted Trail

Editing provided by: Kathleen H. McCormick

Paperback Edition
ISBN-13: 978-0692305225
ISBN-10: 069230522X

Cover Design: L. Sydney Fisher

Author's Note

All names and some locations have been changed in this book for the sake of privacy and out of respect for the deceased. Waking the Dead, Part II of the Bradford Series was inspired by true events. When appropriate the author has dramatized some scenes in this book for the sake of storytelling.

For

Anna & Timothy

CHAPTER 1

Spring, 1860

Henry Lynch pushed the blade of the shovel hard against the grassy earth. As he tossed the dirt to the side, he stared into what would be the fourth grave he had dug in the last three months. His face wore the effects of hard field work endured over the last ten years. His body was tired. His spirit defeated. How could anyone suspect that he was responsible for little Annie's death? But people were talking. Talking about things they knew nothing about.

Frances Williams watched her master through a peephole in the back section of the cabin that she called home. Mr. Henry Lynch had purchased her from a slave owner near DeSoto County, Mississippi. She was known as a troublemaker for ole' man Williams, a busy body who kept things stirred up amongst the other fifty-six slaves he owned. But Henry Lynch thought she was a good investment. And he was right. She was a good worker and tended to her duties without much need for direction. She was a runaway, now beyond child bearing years, and she had a lame foot. She was no good for field work, but she was a great cook and could tend to household duties. And he believed that she was a bargain buy for two hundred dollars.

As Frances quietly observed Henry digging the grave, she trembled with fear as she realized that Master Lynch could have easily killed her instead of Annie. All those white men were "devils" who wielded their power by abusing others. They only loved the bottle and fed off their insatiable sexual desires, even if it meant hurting their own families. Yes, they were "devils". She chewed her fingernails contemplating how he must have managed to kill the child. He had drowned the other three infants. She was sure of it. Three babies don't just die overnight for no reason. They had the fever, but it was Henry Lynch who had taken their lives. And Annie? He must have hit her with the shovel he was using to bury her.

Henry carefully stepped into the grave. Frances took a deep breath as she leaned closer to the opening in the wall of the cabin. *What was he doing now? Why was he moving the body around like that? He had to be hiding something! Maybe it was a knife he had used to stab her.*

Henry placed the small, velvet pouch close to Annie's chest. He stared down at the child and mumbled to himself. Only he knew what he was saying or thinking. As he grabbed the shovel and began to toss the fresh earth upon his lifeless child's body, a shadow emerged and began to surround him.

It was the shadow of something more sinister than any human had ever imagined or realized. It was the reason his family had suffered. The reason his land was cursed. The same land in which now lay his dead daughter. And, as he turned and looked into the face of the evil standing before him, Henry Lynch let out his final cry.

Spring, 1978

Anna Houston snuggled deep into the covers of her bed. The softness of the sheets and the fresh, clean smell soothed her into lucidity. She had survived three hellish months at Lindenwood. She and her family had found refuge in a small home that Natalie had purchased just weeks after her escape from Devon Bradford.

The new home was nestled in a quiet, rural neighborhood surrounded by a cattle farm and acres of cornfields. She was fortunate to have found a great place for her family, something perfect for the right price. She knew nothing of the area's history, nothing about the land upon where her new home now rested. Natalie believed life was finally turning around for her; she was especially optimistic. She hadn't received any annoying or frightening phone calls from Devon Bradford in months, not since he had decided to re-marry.

Anna slept peacefully, her breathing a soft purr in the stillness of the room. Timothy was just across the hall and Natalie slept soundly in the master suite situated between the two children's rooms. They were all near to each other now unlike what had been the layout in the Lindenwood mansion. If anything unusual were to happen here, they would all surely know it. Unless, of course, an unseen predator was capable of moving from room to room without it being noticed. After all, this predator was not of this dimension. And there was, in fact, more than one. Trapped entities. Souls lingering on a land they had once inhabited.

The land had not been cleansed of its former history. There had been bloodshed here. Tragedy and loss. And where there is bloodshed, there are blood stains marking the soil. The life force's resonating mark. The land must be cleansed or it will forever harbor the spirits of its inhabitants.

Footsteps. Heavy footsteps down the hall. The sound of a man wearing boots.

Thump. Thump. Thump.

The entity stopped, confused yet curious of what was behind the closed door. Slowly the door eased open. Just enough to expose Anna's vulnerable sleeping state. She never heard its approach. The shadowy figure stood still, nothing more than a pulsating band of energy as it watched a young, eight-year-old Anna. The room filled up with its presence. Then just as quickly as it had appeared, it faded into the darkness leaving not even a remnant of its pulse.

Anna jolted awake. She pulled the covers up closer to her face as she stared into the darkness. She was disoriented. Had she been dreaming? To what had she suddenly awakened? Memories flooded her mind as she remembered how terrified she felt each time the invisible visitors entered her mother's room at Lindenwood. She knew that she had not been alone in the room. Someone or something had been watching her.

She took a deep breath and settled back against the pillow. She was safe now. She just knew it. But she had awakened a gift, or was it a curse? And had they unknowingly taken residence in another haven of restless spirits, or had her family become susceptible to the occurrence simply by their association with another haunting? How else could it be explained, that unmistakable feeling that her aloneness was suppositious?

The dead had awakened, their quiet and stubborn lingering now interrupted by the breath and reverberation of their former home's new inhabitants. And now, in another time and place, hell was coming.

CHAPTER 2

Natalie Houston wiped the sweat from her forehead as she continued to unload boxes in the blistering July heat. She piled the boxes of clothes and household items in the hall of her new home.

"Where do you want these, Mama?" Timothy stood in the doorway, his arms hugging two stacked and unlabeled boxes, anxious to finish his part of the moving job. He was eager to explore the wooded areas of the property and the old log cabin he had spotted earlier.

Natalie turned around from where she stood at the end of the hallway and looked for an open space to put more boxes. She pointed to the kitchen area at the end of the hall. "I guess you can start stacking them there. How many are left?"

"Two. Can I do something else now?" Timothy pushed his glasses against his face.

"Yeah, go on. I knew you wouldn't last long."

Timothy ignored his mother's remarks as he hurriedly walked out the door. He grabbed one of two machetes used to chop high brush and tree limbs that he had placed by the front door. He kept the large sword-like knives for special expeditions since living in the country meant any day might be spent exploring the rural Mississippi hills.

"Where're you going?" Anna sat on the front porch just outside the front door. She looked at her brother with curiosity, hoping that he would invite her along.

"None of your business."

"Why not?" Anna angrily retorted. Her hands rested on her hips as she stared at her brother's back which began to fade between the bushes.

"Mom said you couldn't go. You better get inside. She said you had to finish helping her unpack. She said I could go." Timothy called over his shoulder never bothering to turn around.

"She did not." Anna huffed and mumbled to herself as she walked back inside the house. She hated being left out of her brother's adventures. He had been her only playmate for the first four years of her life. She couldn't understand his hesitancy now when it came to her tagging along.

Timothy approached a fence of overgrowth separating their property from another house. He aimed his machete at the thick branches of brush, swinging it high and low. The clinking sound of the blade echoed with each blow as the leaves and small branches fell to the ground. He climbed over the pile of greenery and stepped into the backyard of his new neighbor. He stood still as the front of an old, log cabin stared back at him, its front windows dark as if it had a face that now watched him with its own degree of curiosity.

The windows on the cabin were divided by an exterior hall characteristic of nineteenth century homes where two families shared one dwelling. The hall served as a divider and breezeway between the two units. Timothy breathed deeper with amazement as he gazed from a distance. His feet slowly inched forward as he glanced all about the lot on which the cabin rested. A well house stood in view to the left of the cabin, and he could see what looked like the remains of a brick chimney still standing to the right of the cabin.

Timothy's steps became eager as he jumped onto the front porch and paced the length of the cabin while staring intently at the placement of each log. The windows were still intact except for a pane or two missing from the impact of a few BB gun pellets. The right side of the cabin consisted of a living area that looked like an old kitchen with a blue, floral pattern covering the linoleum floor. At the fireplace, smoke stains covered much of the inside of the chimney from numerous meals warmed by the fire's heat. The cabin's age was evident in the musty smell that now lingered here and filled Timothy's nose as he peered out the back window of the room. An unsettling silence loomed about the cabin as if a thousand ears were waiting to hear him speak.

Just outside, Anna was careful not to make a sound in the grass as she sneaked past the front window of the cabin. She saw her brother peering out the back glass and snickered to herself as she planned her strategy of startling him. She gently eased one foot upon the front porch and hunched down low, careful not to stand up in her brother's view. She stayed bent down and waddled to the entrance of the kitchen, peeking around the door. As she stood up, she raised her hands in the air and shouted with all her might, lunging forward into the room as Timothy jumped back and stumbled across the floor. His face was pale with fright but quickly reddened as his anger got the best of him.

"Anna, don't do that. I could have hurt you, idiot!"

Anna giggled. "Did I scare you?"

"Of course not."

"Oh, yes, I did. You jumped ten feet in the air. I saw it."

"Just shut up. Why are you here, anyway?"

"Mama said I could go play. What are you doing?" Anna ignored Timothy's tone and walked over to the window where he had been standing. She leaned forward and looked out the glass.

"What were you looking at? That little house?"

"That's not a house. It's an outhouse."

"What's an outhouse?"

"It's what people used to use before they had bathrooms. Now, stop asking questions."

Timothy walked out of the room and jumped off the porch. Anna followed closely behind him. He walked to the edge of the cabin and stood still as he gazed at a wellhouse with tools and clothes still hanging inside the covered shed.

"Wow, look at that well. It's still open. And someone's coat is still hanging underneath the shed." Timothy exclaimed.

He bent down and picked up a stick and pitched it into the well. The sound of the wood hitting the bottom of a dried hole echoed from its opening. Splinters of wood lay along the opening to the well, and the pitch, black darkness of its depth warned of its danger.

Anna leaned closer to the edge and felt a sense of foreboding. Visions of children falling into the well raced through her mind, and she wondered if anyone had ever died there. Her experience at Lindenwood had followed her here as she now feared the dead and their resentments and intentions. She quickly backed away from the well and walked toward the outhouse shed that stood to itself amongst the tall, dry grass. She pulled on the door several times until Timothy appeared behind her. Though she had expected her brother, she felt startled and cold.

"Let me. There's a nail holding the door shut, dummy."

Anna backed away and watched her brother pull the door open without any effort. He was tall enough to reach the bent nail that she wasn't able to see, let alone maneuver.

Timothy peered inside to find a wooden box of dingy, yellow newspapers. The man-made toilet was nothing more than a deep hole covered by a wood plank with an opening cut to fit the size of the hole. He pulled the box containing the newspapers out of the door and began to shuffle through them as if he were in search of treasure. Anna rushed to his side and began her own sideline exploration.

"Wow, look at this! Bonnie and Clyde are on the front page." Timothy's eyes were big, his eyebrows raised high.

Anna looked strange. "Who are Bonnie and Clyde?" She had heard the names before and wondered if he was referring to the two robbers she had learned of in a movie.

"You know. Those two bank robbers who were killed. We've watched the movie a hundred times." Timothy's tone expressed annoyance.

Timothy examined the year on the newspaper. It read 1934. His eyes widened with interest again as he glanced over the front page of the paper. The cabin had to be older than the 1930's. He threw the paper down and ran toward the broken pieces of brick scattered beneath the chimney's outside wall. He reached down and picked up one of the bricks examining the Fisher name etched into the side of the brick. It was unlike the brick used to build their house. This brick was solid and seemed heavier.

"I bet this place is over a hundred years old." He whispered to himself. He silently wondered who the family was that had owned the cabin and the property and what might have happened to them.

Anna, uninterested in digging through newspapers, wandered about the yard. She skipped through the grass surveying a neatly piled stack of logs, a surplus from the cabin's construction. A narrow brook ran the length of the backyard, and Anna was eager to feel the water's temperature. She began to remove her socks when Timothy walked hastily past her. She turned her eyes in his direction and saw the remains of a white gate covered with vines. With one sock already off, she quickly grabbed it from the ground and slipped it back on and then both of her shoes. She ran after Timothy.

"What is it?" Anna stopped to catch her breath.

Timothy pushed on the gate. Its wooden frame was dry and brittle, the paint chipped and peeling off from years of exposure to harsh weather. He climbed over the gate and started to chomp the tall grass and thickets when he stumbled to the ground.

"What the heck?" Timothy grumbled to himself. He stood up and pointed his machete at the ground moving the grass away from the stone that had apparently caused his fall.

As Timothy cleared the grassy roots from the stone, he discovered that he was standing on top of a long forgotten family graveyard covered by decades of dirt and overgrowth. His blade was fierce and unyielding as he attempted to uncover each stone. Anna watched with amazement and dread as she remembered the graves she had seen through the upstairs window of the Lindenwood mansion. She began to chew her fingernails.

"Timothy, let's go. I don't like this anymore." A slight chill crept up Anna's back as she turned and started for home. An eerie presence seemed to circle her as if it was taunting and waiting to devour her.

Timothy ignored Anna as he continued to slice away at the thick, grassy overgrowth until his effort finally produced the headstones of four unidentified graves. But what he couldn't see was the grave of a seven-year old girl and the multiple graves of three infants buried just steps away in the corner of the cabin's lot. He couldn't hear the girl's distress as she whimpered eternally from the grave and watched Timothy and Anna trespassing on her playground while her father stood tight lipped at the corner of the front porch, his fists clinched at his sides and his translucent face screwed up in anger as he silently observed the two young intruders.

Anna called for Timothy repeatedly. She beckoned for him to follow her and leave the aged graves alone. Her power of discernment was quickly maturing since she had left Lindenwood. She no longer questioned her sense of those darker elements of the unknown. She was just a few months away from turning nine years old now, and she had little trouble accepting the unexplained as a part of the complexity of everyday life. She had already witnessed things that most adults were convinced aren't possible. She watched nervously as Timothy walked from the cabin's lot. As he got closer to her and further away from the cabin, a flood of relief swept over her.

Timothy swung his machete at the ground as he trudged through the tall grass toward a neighboring house. An elderly woman sat in a swing on her front porch while her husband tended to an eight-row garden they had planted in their side yard. Timothy approached the laborious man who was dressed in black cotton pants and a white t-shirt. The dark brown hat he wore was pulled down close to his eyes shielding the sun's scorching rays. He hummed an unknown tune to himself as he diligently hoed weeds from the vegetable plants.

"Hello." Timothy stopped near the garden's edge. He waited for the man to look up.

The man lifted his hat and looked in Timothy's direction. "Hi, there young man. Who are you?"

"I'm Timothy Houston. We just moved in that house next door." Timothy pointed to the end of the drive.

"Oh, you did? Well, it's nice to meet you, Timothy. I'm Jack Adams, but you can just call me 'Mr. Jack'. Who else lives with you?"

Timothy smiled. "My mother and my sister."

Jack propped up against his hoe. "That's a mighty big knife you got there. You like to hunt?"

Jack pointed to the machete Timothy held close to the ground.

Timothy nodded and raised the machete, examing its size. "Sometimes. But normally, I just take this along when I'm walking through tall grass. I was looking around that old cabin over there. Heck, that must be a hundred years old." The excitement in Timothy's voice was evident.

Jack was quiet as he stared in the direction of the cabin. "Yep. It's old alright. I'd guess a couple hundred years. Me and my old lady rented the place for a few weeks back in the 1940's."

Timothy's eyes widened. "You did?"

"Yeah. I don't know who built the place. We didn't stay there long." Jack's tone left Timothy wanting to know more, but the old man's expression indicated his reluctance to say anything further.

Timothy wondered if he knew about the graves. He looked sideways at Mr. Jack as he probed his new neighbor. "Mr. Jack, did you know there were graves over there, a whole bunch?"

Jack cleared his throat. He bent over resting his hands on his knees with his eyes directly in front of Timothy's face. "Son, those graves have been there for years. Forty years ago when I found that place, there was an old, worn-out fence all around those graves. A whole family is buried over there. There's also a little girl and three babies buried in that yard."

"Really? What happened to them?" Timothy's curiosity was overwhelming.

Jack shook his head. "I don't know about that. But, you'd do wise to stay away from over there. I heard this whole area used to be worked by slaves, and it ain't smart to disturb the dead."

Timothy's skin crawled. His hair stood up on the back of his neck as he remembered the place from which he had just moved a few months ago. Lindenwood had swarmed with the restless spirits of Liz and Caroline Bradford. Was that what he had done to Caroline Bradford by moving into her old bedroom? Had he disturbed the dead? But, he couldn't have. She didn't seem angry. She seemed desperate, calling out to him for help every night, disturbed in her own unrest.

"Yeah, You're right. I just thought it was a neat place over there." Timothy started to turn when Jack extended his hand for a handshake.

"Stop by anytime, son." Jack's tone was warm, and the grip of his handshake confirmed his invitation.

Timothy started to walk away and toward his home as Jack pulled his hat low to his forehead and got back to hoeing weeds. Timothy stopped short of crossing into his own yard when he turned and looked back at the man he had just met. He stared at the man and thought hard about his warning. The last thing Timothy wanted was to re-live another Lindenwood. But what if the whole area was a burial ground? He knew his mother well enough to know that she would never have researched the property she had just bought. She had no reason to. Until now.

✝

CHAPTER 3

Anna busied herself hanging clothes in her new bedroom closet. As she studied the organization of her things, a child's laughter echoed in her ear, interrupting the silence. She spun around startled and stood frozen in the doorway of her closet. Her eyes zipped quickly around the empty room searching for the body from which the voice came from, at the same time afraid of what she might see. She was sure that the laughter had belonged to a child.

Then a muffled voice called out to her by name. One voice turned into two as Anna witnessed a garbled conversation. The voices were coming from the hall just outside her room. Her skin began to crawl. Anna frowned. *This must be one of Timothy's pranks.* She rushed to the door flinging it open.

"Okay, Timothy. You can come out now. I know it's you." Anna shouted. Her hands rested on her hips as she waited to hear her brother's laughter, but Timothy never appeared and the mumbling had ceased as quickly as she had opened the door.

Anna's face was pale, her eyes moist. She knew something wasn't right, but why? She whispered a prayer that her new house wouldn't be like Lindenwood.

Ruth Madison drove her 1975 Lincoln Town car around the sharp curve that led to the dead end where her new brick home sat nestled behind a tree-covered lot adjacent to the 150-year old cabin. She and her daughter, Joann had only been living in the house for two weeks before Natalie had joined the neighborhood.

Before leaving for the third trip to the grocery store, Ruth had lifted the kitchen chairs off the floor, turning them upside down and placing them on the table so she could push her mop across the barely soiled area. This had been her routine for years. She was an immaculate housekeeper and mopped her kitchen floors with lemon floor cleaner every two or three days. It was typical of her to leave the house to run daily errands while the floor dried.

Joanne stared out the window of the car as Ruth drove past the cabin. A young girl caught her eye as the car neared the edge of the cabin's yard. The girl was dressed in a flowing, white dress with pink ribbons tied in her long, blond hair. She skipped around the pile of old logs, dancing in a circle as if she had played there many times. Joann sat up tall in her seat and began to roll down her window in an effort to see the girl more clearly.

"Hey, Mama. Who is that little girl?" Joann glanced at her mother and pointed in the direction of the cabin.

Ruth pressed against the car's brakes and looked toward Joann. "What girl?"

Joann jerked around, pointing her index finger to the glass of the passenger side window. "That girl over by the-Where is she? Where did she go? She was just there!"

Ruth disregarded her daughter's remarks as she parked the car, stepped out onto the driveway, and then opened the trunk to gather her groceries. With two bags in her arms, she walked to the back door and carefully inserted her key as she twisted the doorknob and pushed the door open.

Suddenly, Ruth shrieked and fell backwards gasping for breath. Her eyes were wide with astonishment. She steadied herself by the doorframe.

Joann, having stepped out of the car, slammed the car door shut and rushed to her mother's side. "Mama, What's wrong?!"

Ruth's voice was high and frightful. "My kitchen chairs! I placed them on the table before I left…" Ruth trailed off and shuddered. Joann looked away from her mom and through the doorframe at the kitchen chairs scattered around the table.

Joann's brow furrowed and her mouth flew open. "You never forget to put the chairs up, Mama." Joann stood still studying the table and chairs as if they could communicate with her. She knew her mother's routine well, and there was no way that Ruth would have done anything different after fifteen years.

Ruth moved slowly from where she had leaned against the doorframe, picking up the two bags of groceries that she had in tow and entered the kitchen still perplexed by the incident. *Had someone been in her house while they were gone? The door was clearly locked and secure before they had entered. Nothing appeared unusual from the outside.* She tried to brush her uneasiness aside as she made her way back outside to the trunk of her car.

Joann walked into the living room and peered out the front window in search of the mysterious young girl who had played by the cabin and who had vanished almost as soon as she had appeared. The sheer curtain panels blocked very little sunlight from entering the room as her eyes focused on the cabin's lot. She saw her mother walking toward the trunk of the car and realized she still needed help with the groceries. As she started to go, she glanced at her mother once more and this time more closely. The blood drained from Joann's face. Her limbs went weak and her voice was lost as she stood in horror seeing the outline of a man walking with an unyielding determination, almost angrily toward her mother. He was dressed in a long, black coat and carried an ax in his right hand which he had now lifted high above his head. It looked as if he was ready to sling the ax at her unsuspecting mother's head. Right then, Joann bolted from the door and found her voice as she screamed with all her strength.

"Mama, look behind you! A man!" Joann struggled to catch her breath as she rushed from the living room to the trunk of the car.

"What?" Ruth jerked around to find nothing except the sudden flight of a flock of birds in a nearby tree.

Joann looked all around the carport area. "I saw him, Mama. I know what I saw. There was a man who was coming up behind you. He had an ax! What is going on?" Her body trembled as she walked to the edge of the carport, looking all around the property for any sign of the man she had just seen. Like the young girl playing by the cabin, he had simply vanished.

Ruth's eyes were filled with fright and worry. Was she now living in a dangerous place? Or, was there some sort of malignant energy surrounding their new home? Her skin turned cold at the thought of an angry spirit towering over her with an ax. Her mind raced with theories about the family that once occupied the 150-year old cabin. Ruth rubbed her face and held her cheek in her hand. She hugged Joann who snuggled close to her mother's side. Whatever had just attempted to frighten her away would have to do better than that. She wasn't going anywhere. The house and lot she had just bought was the best she had done for herself in years, and she didn't intend to flee because of an unsettled spirit.

CHAPTER 4

As night fell over the neighborhood, Anna organized her bed for sleeping. She pulled the blankets back and placed her two favorite stuffed animals next to her pillow. She walked over to the window and peered out the glass. A giant oak tree towered over the left side of the yard creating a cave of darkness as the sound of diesel truck engines hummed from the nearby highway. Thousands of crickets chirped in unison. Anna pulled the window shade down until it touched the windowsill. A strange feeling of isolation seemed to shadow the property that she and her family now called home.

She felt a sense of unease as she turned off the overhead light and climbed into bed. She wondered if her paranoia was simply a reminder of her days at Lindenwood, or if her feelings of unease were justified.

Anna lay in the darkness, her eyes fixed on the ceiling. Only the soft glow from a wall nightlight provided illumination. As she slowly closed her eyes, she whispered the same prayer she had said every night since leaving Lindenwood.

"Now I lay me down to sleep. I pray, Dear Lord, my soul to keep. If I should die before I wake, I pray, Dear Lord, my soul to take. Amen." Anna nestled deep under the blankets with the two stuffed bears close to her chest. She began to drift into lucidity until the heavy footsteps of a sinister presence filled the hallway.

The pounding of the steps on the concrete floor sounded like the steps of a thick-soled work boot on a hardwood floor. Anna rolled over and sat up on her elbows, her eyes barely open as she squinted to see through the dark room. Who could be coming down the hall wearing work boots? Her bedroom door stood wide open. Anna's pulse began to quicken as she heard the footsteps stop just short of her bedroom entry. She tried to make out a shape or a shadow.

She felt an invisible pair of eyes leering at her through the darkness. An aura of anger and mischief filled the room. Anna lay back on the bed, frozen with fear. She struggled to scream but was unable to mutter a sound even in terror as she watched the doorway expecting the presence to come closer. A strange ball of light began to flicker through the window shade. The light danced the length of the window bouncing up and down as if in rhythm to music. Then, the hammering began, a loud incessant hammering against the brick of the outside windowsill.

Anna jumped from the bed and dashed out the door. She ran across the hall to Natalie's room and pushed the door open. Her mother was in a deep sleep, breathing heavy against the pillow. Anna reached for Natalie's shoulder and shook her hard.

"Mama, wake up. Please. There's something outside my bedroom window." Anna pleaded with urgency. Natalie barely stirred.

"Mama, wake up! Please!" Anna raised her voice.

Natalie rolled onto her back and slowly opened her eyes. "What is it, Anna?"

"Someone or something is outside my window. I'm scared." Anna sat on the corner of Natalie's bed.

Natalie swung her legs over the bed and reached in her bedside table for the revolver that Sarah had given her months ago. She put her hand over her mouth and motioned for Anna not to talk anymore. She tiptoed to the corner of the door and quietly walked into Timothy's room where she recruited her son to join her in the hallway. The house was silent. The hammering had stopped, and as Natalie peered into Anna's room, she saw nothing of the mysterious lights that her daughter had just witnessed dancing in the window.

"Do you want me to check outside?" Timothy barely raised his voice as loud as a whisper while pointing to the door. He carried a small flashlight.

Natalie shook her head. "Look out the window first. Somebody might be out there."

Timothy shined the light at the floor sending a narrow beam of light down the hall and into the living room. He tiptoed to the front window and flicked off the light. He pulled back the curtain and glanced out the window to find nothing and no one other than the two chocolate labs that Natalie had recently adopted. Charlie and Susie lay close together, their heads resting on each other's body. Timothy turned to face Natalie in the hall. He flicked the flashlight on again and shined it toward his mother now standing in the living room.

"I don't see anything." Timothy explained. "Charlie and Susie are sleeping right here under the front porch window. They aren't even barking. If someone was walking around the house, they would have let us known by now." Timothy flicked the flashlight off and started toward the hall.

Natalie nodded, but she wasn't sure and still didn't feel safe. The memory of Lindenwood was too fresh. What if Devon Bradford was up to his old tricks? What if he thought she had something to do with James's drug arrest? She had heard that Devon had moved from the area, but he had accomplished at least one of his goals concerning her. He had instilled fear in Natalie's heart. She was still afraid of what he might do. Natalie held the revolver in her hand and walked steadily to the back door. She unlocked the door and pushed it open calling for the two dogs to come inside. If anyone was trying to come in on her and her family, the dogs would hear it first and alert her.

Charlie, a soft, brown Labrador retriever with a shiny coat and a happy go-lucky personality trotted to the backdoor and into the house. His friend, Susie followed closely along as she always did wherever

Charlie went. Anna sat down in the floor and began to pet the dogs as she waited for her mother to assure her that the ghost was gone.

Natalie shut the door and locked it tight while Timothy started for his room.

"Mama, can I sleep with you for the rest of the night? Please?" Anna implored.

"Alright, come on."

Natalie followed Anna down the hall to her bedroom. They closed the door and locked it before getting into bed. They nestled under the sheets and closed their eyes. Sleep slowly overshadowed them while Charlie and Susie concentrated on the movement of a ghastly presence now lingering in the doorway to Natalie's room. Susie's shackles rose straight up as she jumped to her feet and snarled showing her teeth through the dimly lit hall. Charlie stared without commitment while Susie growled and trembled. Her growls turned into loud, impassioned, warning barks as she readied herself to attack.

Natalie's eyes shot open from a light sleep. Goose bumps covered Natalie's body as she jumped from the bed and rushed to the bedroom door, slamming it shut. She heard the same footsteps that Anna had heard just minutes before. And the steps became louder, heavier, clomping down the hall as if in a mad frenzy to reach her. Anna sat up now in the bed and watched in horror as her mother stood to the side of the door pointing the pistol in the direction of the sound. Next door, Timothy lay motionless in his bed, afraid to make a sound.

"Who's there?" Natalie spoke and waited in silence.

The footsteps stopped. Natalie felt the presence of someone standing at the door waiting to barge through. She motioned for Anna to get down on the floor close to the wall. Her body tensed as she tightened her finger against the gun's trigger pull. Suddenly, what could only be a hand, twisted the doorknob from the outside. The locked door refused to open and the anger of the unseen presence intensified as it forcibly twisted the knob.

Natalie screamed and pulled the trigger. She fired the gun twice in desperation. The bullets shot through the door. Splinters of wood scattered in the doorframe of Anna's bedroom. An eerie silence fell over the house. Natalie was afraid to open the door, not knowing who was waiting on the other side. She hesitantly put her ear to the door and heard nothing. No one was there. At least no one she could hear.

Timothy peeked out into the hall. "Mama, you okay?"

Natalie opened the door. Anna jumped up from the floor and rushed to her mother's side. Natalie put her arm around Anna and reached for Timothy to pull him close. "I'm okay. Did you hear those footsteps?"

Timothy nodded. "Yeah, but where did they go?"

Natalie whispered and shook her head as she inspected the splinters of wood now lying on the floor. "I don't know." She carried the gun close to her side as she walked with her children throughout the house. Charlie and Susie ran frantically in circles still whimpering.

Anna stood back and watched her mother and brother as they inspected each window and door only to find everything locked and bolted as they had left it. She chewed her fingernail and stared around the house studying the rooms as if there was a dark secret hidden behind the walls. In her mind, that's exactly what she would find there behind the walls, in the floors, and on the ceiling. She knew she wasn't imagining what had just happened to her and her family. It was like Lindenwood had followed her, and this time the spirit was seeking her and not Timothy. Anna didn't know enough about spirits to be prepared for what she feared would eventually be facing her. If ghosts were real, she had to know more and if her new home was haunted, she would find out why.

CHAPTER 5

Natalie struggled to rest peacefully after the encounter with the invisible and unwelcome visitor. She tossed and turned for most of the night as she lay in bed under emotional distress, frightened and worried for herself and her children. Who would want to hurt her now? Why was this happening again? She had left Devon Bradford alone. Though she still thought of his youngest daughter, Audrey and prayed for her well-being, she had not had any contact with the Bradford's since leaving. There was no reason for Devon Bradford to torment her. He had quickly moved on.

That morning, Natalie stretched and yawned as she quickly got dressed. She grabbed her purse and called to Anna who patiently sat on the sofa. Still feeling uneasy about the night's happening, Natalie slammed the door behind her as she and Anna rushed to the car.

Her mind raced as she drove Anna into town. She thought about what her own next steps should be concerning the recent disturbances. Should she research the property to find out the history and who had lived there? Was there any point in doing that? She could just ignore the whole thing. But, that's not how it happened at Lindenwood. No amount of apathy could have eased the anguish of Liz Bradford's spirit.

Natalie pulled into a nearby parking lot. The vinyl seats of the Oldsmobile were blistering hot from the mid-August sun. Anna climbed off the front seat with caution. She had been able to persuade Natalie to stop by the downtown library. She didn't tell her mother why she was so adamant about checking out books on that particular day, and Natalie never seemed to notice the urgency in Anna's request.

Anna searched the card catalog. She scribbled her selection down on loose slips of paper and then walked to the section of the library where she was promised to find at least three books about ghosts. She ran her fingers along the outside row of books while her eyes skimmed over the numbers. Her fingers stopped short when her eyes became fixed on a title of a book about witchcraft. Anna quickly pulled the book from the shelf and flipped it open. She skipped through the pages as if searching for answers to questions she wasn't sure to ask and then continued her search along the shelf until she pinpointed a small, thick book on the paranormal. She walked to the checkout counter and handed the clerk her library card. The fresh smell of ink and the machine's hum as it stamped each card hypnotized Anna as she stared out the front window.

"Here you go. They're due back in two weeks." The mousy brown-haired clerk smiled politely at Anna and handed the books over the counter.

"Thanks." Anna took the books and walked briskly out the door.

Natalie had been watching through the library's front window as Anna finished checking out her books. She puffed on a cigarette and glanced down at her watch. It was just after 1:00 p.m., and only a couple of hours before she had to report to work. Natalie had taken a nursing position closer to home after leaving Lindenwood. She missed seeing her friend, Margaret, at North Mississippi Medical Center, but she didn't miss working the long weekends or the thirty-minute drive to work. She still talked to Margaret by phone and made time to visit with her when she was in the Tupelo area, but over the past few weeks Natalie had become acquainted with a co-worker who was a Native American Indian.

Natalie was immediately drawn to the olive-skinned woman for her unusual and descriptive recollections of the Sioux customs. The short, petite woman's hands were long and slender, her eyes set deep as in the depths of a dark cave. She was known only by her nickname "Meda" to most people, and unless she removed her veil of caution, no one was allowed to know her any closer. But, Natalie was one of Meda's chosen, a sort of kindred spirit. Meda saw the stirrings of Natalie's heart, the past pains and future dreams. She was gifted in that respect. Unlike Natalie's habit of discounting her psychic side, Meda entertained hers and was regarded by her inner circle as an authority on the spirit world with a renowned gift of clairvoyance.

While Natalie chauffeured Anna across town, Timothy was busy entertaining himself. It wasn't long before he had found his way into the wilderness of the subdivision. He carried his .22 rifle and machete close to his hip after a long afternoon of hunting in the woods. He rarely went on expeditions in search of anything in particular but merely hunted whatever crossed his path.

As Timothy walked out of the dark wooded area, he noticed the sun's light illuminating his path. The forest's shadow had fooled him into thinking that nightfall was upon him. He neared the edge of the woods when he snatched his rifle close at the sound of a commanding, screech coming straight at his head. He stared in the path of the sound and jumped down just before an owl barely missed his face. The owl's legs were stretched forward. Its talons were spread out and ready to attack. Its eyes were fixed, dark and determined as it came toward Timothy. Just as Timothy avoided the owl's attack, it landed on a low tree branch and fell to the ground. Its wings flapped and beat against the hard ground desperate to escape from its own fate.

"Damn! What the hell was that?" Timothy shouted to himself.

Timothy rushed to the owl's side and stared at the small bird as it gasped for breath. He knelt down beside the bird and scooped it into his hand. He was awestruck as he beheld the mysterious bird of night, a creature few ever actually saw in the wild. He had read about owls and their almost supernatural ability of sight and hearing. Their weird ability to twist their head in a complete circle always reminded him of that scene in The Exorcist. It was a frightening sight to see, an inexplicable skill unlike any other animal.

Timothy was almost a mile from home. He ran most of the way, stopping only to rest his lungs before he picked up his speed again. If he could get home and get a vet's help, he might be able to save the wild bird. He panted hard as he dropped his machete and rifle to the ground upon entering the corner of his yard. He used both hands to hold the owl and knelt on the concrete floor of the carport. He began to massage the owl's chest, hoping to stimulate a failing heart, but the owl's breathing had stopped and his heart had weakened to its last beat.

Natalie pulled into the drive and saw Timothy standing over what appeared to be a small animal.

She and Anna got out of the car, urgent with curiosity.

"What are you doing?" Natalie watched her son as he continued his resuscitation attempts.

"I thought I could save it. I hoped I could." Timothy's tone was full of disappointment.

Natalie shook her head in disbelief. "And what in the world did you intend to do with an owl?"

"Make it a pet." Timothy answered her as if she had asked an obvious question. He didn't bother looking up.

"Timothy, you can't make a wild animal a pet." She shook her head and started inside the house while Anna examined the owl with amazement.

"Where did you find it?" Anna stepped closer and knelt down, looking at its eyes already fixed open in death.

"It almost hit me. I was in the woods. It must have been hurt before I saw it, because it just fell to the ground."

"Wow, it looks kind of scary to me. What are you going to do with it?" Anna asked.

"I don't know. I think it's cool. I might get it stuffed." Timothy stared upon the now lifeless creature.

Anna snarled her nose and walked inside the house where Natalie was busy changing clothes.

"Your grandmother will be here in a few minutes. She's going to spend the night with us tonight since I won't get off work until 11:00 p.m." Natalie slid on her work shoes.

"Oh, boy! I can't wait to see Grandma." Anna clapped her hands together. She ran for her room and shut the door, intent on studying her new books before her grandmother, Sarah Cooper, arrived. She didn't want anyone to know she was reading about ghosts. If her grandmother caught her with books on witchcraft or the paranormal, she would probably take them away from her and tell her mother.

Anna made a pallet of blankets in the corner of her room, hidden from the door entry. Anna opened the first book on the paranormal and began reading about poltergeists. She had never heard of poltergeists and repeated the words aloud to herself as she read. As she flipped the pages, she ran her fingers across the lines that compared the definitions to hauntings. The occurrences of both phenomena were similar except for the frightening reality that poltergeists were known to be associated with malevolent spirits. Anna's skin tingled all over. Why had the ghostly presence from the evening before chosen to visit her room? Was she the target of an angry spirit? She was too young to understand just how sensitive she was to ghostly presences. Not everyone possessed the same psychic abilities and receptions.

Anna closed the book and stared blankly at the wall. She thought of her family's narrow escape from Lindenwood. Devon Bradford's crazed face and its contortions reeled through her mind like film in a movie projector. She had no doubt that Lindenwood was haunted by the spirits of Liz and

Caroline Bradford, but she trembled at the thought of Devon being possessed by a demonic spirit, though he wasn't dead. She hid the two books under her bed and reached for her Bible from the windowsill. She flipped to the New Testament and began to search for the stories of Christ's exorcisms and then closed the cover and held it close to her chest as she silently whispered a prayer. If there was one thing that terrified Anna Houston, it was the possibility of demonic spirits taking control of her body. Whatever had stood outside her door the night before had not behaved as a ghost of good intent but rather delighted in its ability to scare and confuse. Anna did not feel welcome in her new home.

CHAPTER 6

Natalie sat in silence as she waited for Meda to join her in the cafeteria. She wanted to get Meda's opinion about the recent events. She trusted Meda. There was no one else in whom she could confide. These recent events had to remain secret. If her mother, Sarah Cooper, found out about this she would swear that Natalie was going insane and possibly insist that she see a psychiatrist. Natalie knew that she didn't need a psychiatrist, but she wasn't qualified to handle a haunting either. Whatever was happening to her was unexplainable, certainly not by medical means.

Meda pushed the door open and spotted Natalie sitting alone near a secluded corner of the room. She made her way over to the table after filling her cup with black coffee.

"Hi, Friend." Meda greeted Natalie with a smile as she sat down across from her.

Natalie looked tired, her eyes sunken and dark. She let out a sigh and smiled at Meda. "Hey, I am so glad to see you."

Meda studied Natalie's face. She absorbed her emotions and realized that Natalie was living with some degree of fear. "Natalie, you look drained. What's going on?"

Natalie fidgeted in her seat. "Meda, do you remember me telling you about my experiences at Lindenwood and how I managed to live through that hell?"

"You're speaking of your time with Devon Bradford. Yes, I remember. Go on."

Natalie's eyes began to water. "Something's wrong. Something's bad wrong."

"What do you mean?" Meda studied her.

"Hell, I don't know what I mean. I'm having nightmares. Or, maybe I'm not. I don't know what the hell I mean. It's happening again."

"What's happening? Ghosts?"

"I'm hearing things, Meda. The damn dogs are even acting strange. Staring at something or someone who isn't there."

Meda leaned back in her chair realizing the magnitude of what her friend was telling her. She felt sympathy for Natalie. She knew Natalie and her family had now become susceptible to these occurrences. Not by choice, but by exposure. It was as if a portal had been opened. A bleeding cut in her or through one of her children's auras that could be an opening to an ethereal world.

"You are scared, Natalie. Don't show fear. It thrives off your fear."

"Of course, I'm scared. How the hell did I end up in this situation again? This home has no history, Meda. No one has lived here before us."

"That doesn't matter. The land has a history. If you want to understand what's happening and why, you have to research the land. It has a story and in that story lies the answer to stop what's tormenting you." Meda sipped the coffee savoring the aroma as the liquid moistened her lips.

"So how and where do I begin to do that?"

Meda leaned forward. "Find out who lived on that land. Begin at the beginning."

Natalie looked confused.

"The courthouse, my dear. Search the land records at the courthouse."

"So, I can find the original owners? How will I know about their lives? Specifics?"

"You will have to find the oldest records there. It may take you some time, but if you want this to stop, you have to find out why it's happening."

"I don't understand what you mean." Natalie dropped her head. She picked at her fingernails. She felt defeated.

Meda reached for Natalie's hand giving her a reassuring squeeze. "Don't fret, my friend. I will help you. I must tell you this. The soil of the earth holds a picture of the past. If your land has seen the bloodshed of many, those imprints will still be there. The souls may not rest. The land would need to be cleansed. All of my people knew the importance of cleansing the land before inhabiting it."

"So you're saying that I might be living in an area where people had died a tragic death?"

Meda nodded. "Yes, Or worse."

"Or worse? What do you mean 'worse'?" Natalie was troubled.

"Start your search now, Natalie. Do it now. Do not wait."

CHAPTER 7

Anna loaded her arms with plastic play dishes and dolls of different sizes. Her curiosity had been unleashed upon hearing the story of the cabin and its graves. She was eager to explore the grounds and to make the cabin her new playhouse. She dumped her playhouse necessities into a small red wagon and proceeded to pull it behind her.

She waded through tall grass and brush until she had reached the front of the cabin's clearing. She stood in awe of the cabin's age. Her eyes drifted around the lot as she viewed the wellhouse and the clothes still hanging underneath the shed's roof.

There was a stillness, except for the sound of the wind weaving through the clearing over the cabin. She started for the steps, climbing up to the porch and making her way into the cabin's 'kitchen' room.

Once there, goosebumps covered Anna's arms as she gazed into the ashen stained fireplace equipped with a black hanging cauldron. It still rested in the same spot where it had been used many years before. Her mind raced with visions of a woman wearing an apron and bent over the pot. She wondered about the identity of the previous owners and if they were buried somewhere on the grounds. Were they ghosts haunting the cabin and even the surrounding land that now included her house? She wondered too if they were the ghosts responsible for the noisy footsteps outside of her bedroom every night.

Anna began to arrange her dolls in an old wooden doll bed that she had found during her neighborhood exploration. She was oblivious to the sounds that were creeping up behind her through the outside breezeway. The footsteps had started as a low thump from the opposite side of the cabin.

Now aware of the noise, Anna suddenly froze where she sat, leaning over the doll bed. The sound of heavy footsteps grew louder and echoed through the room. A bone-numbing chill, accompanied by a sense of dread, swept over her as she now stood rigid in the center of the room. She felt the hair rise up on the back of her neck as she slowly looked around the room searching for the source of the footsteps. Anna's skin turned pale, her eyes glazed over, flooded with fear.

"Is someone there?" Anna's voice trembled, and her eyes began to moisten, as if she might cry.

Without warning, a thunderous boom filled the room as a gust of cold air swirled just above her head. Almost simultaneously, the footsteps began to march in rhythm to a silent beat. Anna jumped and screamed as she raced from the room and down the front porch steps. She did not dare look back as she skidded in the loose dirt. She panted and cried taking in giant, hurried gasps of air as she raced to the front door of her home. She jerked the door open and slammed it shut behind her.

Anna rested her hands on her knees as she bent over trying to catch her breath. She began to sob, her whimpers becoming harder and louder.

"I left everything. I can't leave my dolls." Anna spoke aloud. She had left all of her dolls in the cabin, in the 'kitchen' room. How was she going to get the courage to go back? It was the man in the black coat, and he'll be watching me now, she thought. She chewed her fingernail and lifted the curtain as she peered out the back door's window.

She stared at the cabin just a short distance away. As she focused her eyes on the cabin's front broken window, she gasped. Just behind the glass and turned in her direction, stood the outline of a man wearing a wide brimmed hat. She recognized him almost immediately. This was the man who had been visiting her room every night. She was sure of it. But, who would believe her if she were to tell anyone that he was a ghost?   The figure stood very still, studying her.   And even though his eyes were dark, completely hidden, Anna sensed that those eyes were in a deadlock with her own.   What did he want with her?

CHAPTER 8

Natalie skipped up the courthouse steps carrying a notebook and a bag of writing utensils. This would be an expedition for her. She would be acting on Meda's advice and starting her search eager to uncover the secrets of her land. She wondered if Meda's claims would prove true. Had there been bloodshed there?

She approached the front hall and made her way to the Chancery Court records near the back of the building. As she opened the door, she noticed a few women behind a long counter. No one seemed to notice her as she continued past the counter and made her way to the records department.

Natalie stood still for a moment as she studied the room. Row after row of ledgers were neatly filed and stacked along the inner walls. She was overwhelmed by the number of ledger books and wondered how old they might be and where she should begin.

She let out a sigh and placed her things on top of a table. She opened her notebook and found the copy of her land deed that she had brought with her. Natalie glanced along the wall as she slowly walked near what she determined were the oldest files. She pulled one of the ledgers from its case and carefully opened and positioned it on a nearby table. The dingy pages and musty smell indicated its age.

The ledger held records from the early 1800's. Natalie traced her fingers over the century old ink as she examined the entries. She searched for her own land recordings.

"There!" Natalie shouted aloud. She quickly glanced behind her to see if she had disturbed the ladies in the next room. They hadn't noticed her. Natalie turned her attention back to the ledger, and her mouth fell open as she studied the entry.

February 1, 1836. A man by the name of Henry Lynch had acquired the 110 acres of land once occupied by the American Indians following their forced relocation by the government.

"Oh my God!" Natalie whispered to herself as she placed her hand over her mouth. *That would mean that perhaps there were unknown burial grounds on the property. Would anyone have bothered to find out before building a subdivision there? She thought probably not. And, if this were true, there was no doubt in her mind that her land would need to be cleansed.*

Natalie continued to study the records for more information, looking for any more clues, but her efforts proved pointless. Her discovery had only presented her with more questions. She packed her things together and walked quickly out the courthouse doors.

Two hours later, Natalie picked up the phone and dialed Meda. She needed help and Meda had offered. She was relieved to hear her friend's voice on the other end of the line.

"Hello?"

"Hello, Meda. Does that offer of help still stand?"

"Hey, my friend. You know it does. What's going on?"

"I took your advice and went to the courthouse. My land was acquired in 1836 by a man named Henry Lynch. The only problem with all this searching is that I don't know what I am searching for."

"That's just it. You are simply studying the history of your place. Enjoy the journey. Now, the next step should probably be finding out who Henry Lynch was. You are going to have to do some research into his family tree. You might discover some of his distant relatives living in the area."

Natalie sighed. "Well, there is a clue about this property. Henry Lynch was the only person on record who ever owned the land. The records were dated 1836 which could mean that my land was not owned prior to the removal of the Indians. Do you realize what this means? My land could be the resting place of hundreds of Native Americans.

Meda's voice peaked with interest. "That's right, and if those remains were disturbed, may God help the intruder."

CHAPTER 9

Natalie held her head in her hands gripping handfuls of hair as she struggled to overcome the piercing pain in her stomach. Her abdominal area growled and moaned as if she hadn't eaten in hours, only now with a deep and relentless intensity. Her intestines felt as if they were being twisted apart, and the sensation of thousands of bees stinging her insides caused her to become faint.

She crawled from the living room sofa down to the floor and then through the hall. She pushed the bathroom door open with one hand and continued on her hands and knees to the tub. She turned the handle to hot. As the tub filled with water, a thick steam rose up, and Natalie breathed deeply. She had battled bouts of abdominal distress for the past couple of weeks.

After removing her clothes, she climbed into the tub and massaged her abdomen. The hot water worked to ease her distress. She laid her head back against the tub, the hot water at her neck, and closed her eyes, drifting into a much needed escape.

Timothy finished stacking logs before turning to go inside. Nightfall had started to descend over the house. His nose was red and dripping with sinus drainage from the chilling wind. As he reached for the door, it opened several inches wide as if the wind had swirled it open. He pretended not to notice the incident and walked inside when suddenly he heard the phone's loud and incessant ringing. He sprung toward the phone and grabbed the receiver.

"Hello?" Timothy caught his breath. His back ached from stacking logs.

"Is Natalie home? This is Meda."

"Uh, yes, Ma'am. But, I'm not sure where she is. Can you hold on?"

"Yes, sure."

"Okay." Timothy laid the receiver on the kitchen table and walked down the hall where he found the bathroom door closed.

"Mom, are you in there?" He knocked on the door.

Natalie had felt almost comatose as she lay back in the tub. She opened her eyes. She looked up at the ceiling and cleared her throat. "Yeah, what do you need?"

"Someone's on the phone for you. A woman named Meda."

Natalie took a deep breath. "Okay, tell her I'll be there in a minute." Her fingertips had already begun to wrinkle from the water. She eased out of the tub, grabbing a towel that lay by the sink and quickly toweled off before slipping on a houserobe.

Timothy walked back to the phone. "Ma'am, my mom said she would be here in a minute." He laid the phone on the kitchen table without waiting to hear Meda's response.

Natalie made her way to the kitchen and picked up the phone. She sat down and lit a cigarette. As she exhaled a long, stream of smoke, she raised the receiver to her ear.

"Hello?" Natalie's fatigue and exhaustion was evident in her strained voice.

"Natalie? Hey, are you ok? You sound sick."

"I'm not feeling well, Meda. Sorry I took so long getting to the phone. I was just getting out of the tub. I had to soak in a hot bath."

Meda paused. She had a feeling that something was wrong with Natalie before she even called. She had been feeling uneasy about Natalie's susceptibility to negative influences since Natalie had told her about Lindenwood.

"When did all this start? Was it sudden? You seemed fine a few days ago."

Natalie puffed on her cigarette. "It's just a stomach bug or something that I ate. It comes and goes." Natalie tried to downplay her illness, but Meda wasn't satisfied.

A sense of dread shadowed Meda. Her eyes narrowed and her face became distorted with worry. "Have you been having any weird dreams, or is anything else unusual going on there? I can't help worrying about you, not since our conversation a few days ago."

Natalie cringed. Surely she wasn't being targeted by the curse of Liz Bradford? She had done no wrong to her. So, why would she be made a target? It didn't make sense. If the spirit of Liz Bradford wanted vengeance on anyone, it should be Devon Bradford. Natalie's mind raced, and she was feeling anxious all over again. She thought about the past few days and the noises that she and the children had been hearing.

"I would like to forget about that time in my life. I made a mistake by getting involved with that family. And it's a mistake that might literally haunt me for the rest of my life. But, since you asked- I will tell you that the kids and I woke up a few nights ago to some strange noises. Anna swears she saw a flickering light outside her window. I just thought that it might be some of the neighborhood kids playing a prank, but then I heard the strangest footsteps in the hallway."

"What do you mean by strange?" Meda listened intently.

"Loud, like heavy work boots. The footsteps stopped outside my bedroom door. Needless to say, I was terrified. I couldn't believe that someone might have just walked inside our house. On another night, Anna came to my room and woke me after hearing someone with what might have been a hammer pounding the brick wall outside her bedroom window. That happened before she saw the lights."

"Oh my God, Natalie. Did you find anybody in the house?"

"No, and we looked outside and couldn't find anything or see anyone. But, there's a bullet hole in the wall in the hallway where I shot at whoever or whatever was outside my bedroom door."

Meda's hand flew to her mouth. "You've got to be kidding? And no one was there?"

"No one." Natalie paused and stared at the owl with its wings outstretched and its black eyes fixed in an angry stare. She felt threatened by the owl's stance but couldn't figure out why. Even though the owl was dead and mounted on a wooden plaque, she felt the power of its presence. It seemed almost monstrous as if it hovered over the house.

"That damn bird that Timothy brought in here is giving me the creeps." Natalie tried to change the subject.

Meda felt nauseated. "You said a bird?" Her voice was full of panic.

"Yeah, it was an owl. Timothy said it flew right at him when he was coming out of the woods a few days ago. He tried to save it. You know how he collects wild pets. But it died, and he had it mounted.

So, it's in my living room. I swear that bird is staring back at me. It looks like it's alive."

"Natalie, get that owl out of your house now!" Meda's urgency scared Natalie. She knew that the owl was an omen.

"Why? What do you mean?" Natalie became chilled as goose bumps crept over her body.

"That bird is a bad omen. Owls are symbols of death according to our ancient teachings. Get it out of your house. Get it out, now!"

Natalie's hands begin to tremble. Her stomach churned. "Okay, I will. Right now. But what should I do with it?"

"It really doesn't matter what you do with it after it's out of the house. Put it outside for now. But, do not bring it back into your house."

"Okay, let me go. I'll call you back later. I'm scared." Natalie started to hang up the phone when she heard Meda calling out to her.

"Natalie, listen to me. Don't be scared. Just do what I'm telling you. Everything will get better."

"Okay." She hung up the receiver and turned to look at Timothy staring at her with curiosity.

"Timothy, we have to move your owl for a little while. We need to put it outside."

"Why? I don't want to move it outside. Can't I keep it in my room?"

Natalie shook her head. "I don't think so. I think we'll just have to trust Meda's advice for now."

Timothy looked at his mother with confusion.

"Meda thinks the owl was an omen. A bad one. She says if I take the owl out of the house, my sickness will go away."

Timothy nodded. He didn't bother to question the urgency of his mother's request or what he needed to do. He quickly walked to the wall where the owl was mounted and leaned forward to reach for the plaque. He carried the owl to the outside carport where he placed it on the concrete floor. He imagined it suddenly flying away. As he looked at the owl, he too noticed the liveliness of the dead owl's eyes and the invading energy of its wide stretched wings.

Timothy wondered if removing the owl had also been effective in removing the spirit that he and Anna had encountered over the last few weeks. If there really was a spirit in their new house, he couldn't speak a word of it to Natalie. He couldn't tell her. She might not believe him, but then, what if she did believe him? What if she was experiencing the same things? It would be Lindenwood all over again. So, he would wait. If these and other bizarre events continued, he would have to tell Natalie, but not yet.

CHAPTER 10

Anna read teen magazines behind her bedroom door. She was oblivious to what was happening in the next room. Natalie started for her bedroom. She imagined herself with restored good health and already felt a sense of calm. Perhaps it was all in her head? Surely there wasn't any real truth to Meda's warning, but she couldn't deny that her friend, Margaret, had been right about Lindenwood and Devon Bradford. Natalie longed for normalcy in her life, but it seemed far from her reality. What she did know to be real was the paranormal activity that she had witnessed over the past year.

Timothy reached for the door handle and pushed the back door open from the outside. Flashes of their time at Lindenwood raced through his mind as he entered the house. If the owl had been an omen, he wanted to find out why, and he had a plan for later. After everyone was asleep, he would unwrap the Ouija board that he had been saving for months. He had bought the board game at a local toy store after he had heard from kids at school about the game's accuracy. He wanted to see for himself. If there was a spirit in the house, he wanted to find out. The ghost of Caroline Bradford had frightened Timothy beyond any fear he had ever known, but at the same time, the experience of meeting her ghost had raised his curiosity to a level that shouldn't have ever been awakened.

Anna opened her bedroom door and started for the kitchen. She suddenly froze in the hallway as a gust of icy, cold air rushed past her. The cool blast was strong enough to move her hair away from her face.   Anna had to catch her breath.   She was paralyzed in place.

"What was that?"   Anna rubbed her arms trying to comfort herself.

Timothy stopped in his tracks.   He stared blankly at his sister not sure what she was talking about and fearing to know. "I don't know.   What happened?"

"A gust of cold air just whirled right at me.   It almost knocked me down!"   Anna looked stunned and held her arms close to her chest.

Suddenly, the spirit's rage filled the room as a drinking glass that Natalie had left on a nearby sofa table shattered before their eyes.   Splinters of glass shot across the room in every direction.   Timothy jerked his hands in front of his face as Anna hid around the corner of the wall.   Their mouths hung open and their bodies trembled as they stared at the debris and then at each other.   Both of them stood still and stiff for what seemed like hours.   Finally, they managed to step away from where they hid and pick up the scattered glass.

———————————— ❦ ————————————

It was past 10:30 p.m. The house was quiet and all the lights were out as Anna and Natalie slept soundly across the hall. Timothy stood alone in his bedroom. He unwrapped the cellophane paper from the Parker Brothers board game and placed it on the floor in front of him. He sat down on the floor with his legs crossed Indian style and positioned the board on his knees. He skimmed over the rules of the game and realized he was already breaking one of them; he did not have a second player. If he were able to contact a spirit, it would have to use only him as the portal. It was frightening enough with the use of two players, but to have only one person as a portal through which the entity could speak was not only dangerous but downright madness, he thought. If the entity desired, it could take possession of his body and cause his family more trouble than they ever imagined possible while living at Lindenwood.

A candle flame danced nearby casting just enough light to make out the board's letters and the *yes* or *no* responses that were at the top of the board above the letters. Timothy positioned the plastic planchete on the board and gently placed his fingertips against the part that's shaped like an arrow. He closed his eyes and concentrated on what he wanted to say. Then he mumbled the words aloud.

"I want to speak to someone tonight. Is there anyone out there?"

The planchete sat still. Timothy peeked at it from one eye. He watched the window of the planchete and imagined seeing it move across the board, but it was perfectly still.

"Can you tell me your name?" Timothy waited and then let out a sigh. He concentrated on keeping his fingers still. If the planchete did move, he wanted to be certain that he hadn't caused it himself.

"Is there a spirit in this house?" Timothy felt scared as soon as he asked the question out loud. He opened his eyes upon hearing a hiss from the candle's flame. The flame bounced eagerly as if it had come to life.

Timothy held his breath and then repeated the question, the one he dreaded asking again. He feared that he already knew the truth. "Is there a spirit among us in this house?"

As the planchete sat still, he spoke with more urgency, now demanding an answer. "I want to know, is someone here with us?"

With vigor, the planchete abruptly zipped to the left top corner of the board and Timothy's hands shot up in surprise. The planchete rested there as Timothy tried to compose himself and catch his breath. He stared down at it and saw the word '*Yes*' magnified through the glass circle. His skin crawled as he ventured to challenge the spirit and again placed his fingers upon the planchete.

"Ok, if you're really here, make the lights come on." Timothy hoped he was imagining what had just occurred and hoped the spirit couldn't prove itself. His worst fear would be to find out if it meant him or his family any harm. The spirit of Caroline Bradford never intended to hurt Timothy or his family, but she had caused them enough psychological distress to last a lifetime. He could never forget. At least, so far, this spirit had not shown itself to them.

Timothy removed his fingertips from the planchete. The spirit would have to rely on its own energy to turn the lights on in the room. And, suddenly just as he thought it, the light bulbs above Timothy's head flickered on and buzzed madly. He looked up at the light afraid the bulbs would explode just like the glass. The stereo receiver flashed on and off for a brief moment. Timothy jumped to his feet. He knew the room was full of its energy. He reached for the light switch and flicked it on even though the room was already lit. His breathing was heavy, and his skin was crawling as he stood numbly overlooking the room.

His steps were quick as he walked back to the center of the room and then blew out the candle. He picked up the board and hastily placed it back in its box. If he had any doubts about what he and Anna had heard a few nights before, they were now gone as he realized he was in the very company of someone or something whose presence was strong and purposeful and invisible to the human eye. But that someone or something was capable of seeing and hearing him even when Timothy wasn't aware. He and his family were being watched. And if this spirit could turn on lights, what else could it be capable of?

CHAPTER 11

Natalie had spent the last several days busily uncovering the truth about Henry Lynch's past. She knew he had been a wealthy man before the Civil War, but like many others, he had suffered catastrophic loss during the war and was left with only remnants of an abundant past. Death and destruction overshadowed his homestead during the years following the end of the war. Reconstruction was a word meant for those southern people who had something left to build upon.

They had come upon his place after nightfall. It was during the dark hours that the Union delivered an onslaught of fiery hell. He could do nothing but pray for his family's lives to be spared. He watched as his livestock scattered and his slaves escaped to the forest gaining their freedom if they could survive the wilderness. Frances, the Lynch's house slave clung fiercely to Mrs. Lynch as she and the Lynch children searched for a hiding place in the underground room beneath the staircase. The sound of horse hooves pounding in the front parlor echoed through to every corner of the house.

And then silence filled the air. There were no more indications of a horse's gallop or a soldier's call as he torched another barn on the property. It was quiet, a haunting, sadistic quiet. The women carefully exited their hiding place, leaving the children safely hidden, and stood in horror as they examined the remains of their homestead. Henry Lynch lay slumped against a wall, trickles of blood oozing down his cheeks from the brunt force of a soldier's ferocious attack. He slowly stood, steadying his legs, and surveyed the property through the broken panes of glass. There was only one structure still intact among the ruins. For reasons unknown, the dogtrot cabin on the east side of the property had survived.

Natalie stood watching out the front window. She wondered if the old man next door knew anything about the place. She watched him sitting on his front porch as she tried to decide how best to approach him. What would she say? She couldn't just come right out and tell him that she thought the place was haunted. He would think she was crazy, but she knew she would have to start asking questions of people at some point if she was going to find out more about the land and its history. She still didn't have the answers she needed about Henry Lynch's family. The records had shown that the Lynches lost three infants and one young girl, but nothing pointed to the cause of death. The only way to find out the details of their story would be to find someone who knew it.

Natalie slipped on her socks and tennis shoes and grabbed a notepad and pen. She went through the kitchen to the back door, stepping out into a brisk, cool breeze. She locked the door behind her and headed down the gravel driveway to meet her neighbor next door.

Natalie walked to the corner of her neighbor's yard and hesitated. She cleared her throat and called out to him.

Jack leaned forward in his lawn chair and noticed Natalie. He waved and started to stand.

"Hello. How are you?" Jack called out across the yard.

"I am fine, thank you. I am your neighbor. My name is Natalie. I don't believe we've met."

Jack walked to meet Natalie. He extended his hand for a handshake. "Yes, ma'am. The name is Jack." He offered a toothy smile stained by coffee and tobacco.

"It's nice to meet you, Jack. Hey, I was wondering if you might know anything about this area."

"What do you mean?"

"I wondered if you have lived in this area for many years and if so, maybe you know who lived here before us?"

Jack looked at Natalie curiously. "No one lived here before us. The place was an empty field except for that cabin over there." He pointed in the direction of the cabin.

"Oh ok." Natalie turned to look at the cabin secluded by the numerous tall Oak trees that surrounded the lot.

"About that cabin, it's very old. Makes you wonder how long it's been here." Natalie probed further.

Jack stood very still. He looked down at the ground as if he were studying something buried just beneath it. "Yes, ma'am. That cabin has been there since the mid-1800's. There is a story about that place."

"Really? Can you tell me?" A sense of urgency was apparent in Natalie's voice.

Jack stared back at Natalie, his brow slightly furrowed, as though he knew why she wanted to know. Natalie felt a sense of unease as she realized that her neighbor had information, possibly of a dark sort, that he might be guarding for some unknown reason.

"The Lynch family originally lived there. Ole' man Lynch was once a very wealthy man until sometime after the Civil War. They say he lost his mind and killed his children. The story I always heard growing up was that the place was cursed."

"Oh my God. Cursed by what? Do you know?" Natalie raised her hand to her mouth.

"Ah, it was an old Indian curse. Indians once lived in the area before the Removal in the 1700's. Legend has it that an Indian village once stood here.

The Indians cursed the white man and the land after they were forced to leave."

"But no one knows if that's actually true, right?" Natalie felt an icy chill creeping up her arms.

Jack laughed. "No, nobody knows if that's true. It's just stories. But, I do know those kids are buried on that lot. I lived in that house for a few months back in the 1940's. We weren't there long." Jack's tone was now different and alarming as he emphasized his point.

"Why are you asking about this place?" Jack looked intently at Natalie.

Natalie paused. "I-I've just had some strange things happen around the house since we moved in." Her laugh was noticeably nervous.

Jack looked at her with raised eyebrows. "You too, huh? The Madisons have said the same thing. You know, I saw your kids playing over there a few days ago. If I was you, I would keep them out of there."

Natalie's calmness was fading fast, her composure affected now as her back began to slump. "Yes, sir. I will." She thanked Jack for his time.

As Natalie turned to leave, Jack called out to her. "Ma'am, I just thought of something else. Ole' man Lynch died shortly after his oldest daughter was buried. The story goes that something evil scared that man as he was digging her grave. Nobody knows what it was that he saw, but the story remains to this day that he died of a heart attack after seeing something so evil that it killed him. I wouldn't go over there. In fact, I wouldn't even concern myself with that place anymore if I was you."

Natalie shuddered but nodded. "Thank you, sir." She walked quickly back down the gravel driveway and rushed to the backdoor. She pushed it open and sat down in a nearby chair. Her body trembled as she recounted her conversation with Jack.

Jack had issued a warning to her. His words were direct, but why? What else did he know?

Natalie wondered if he was trying to protect her or if he was trying to protect someone else? But who?

Natalie held her head in her hands. Her mind raced. *This could not be happening again. How in the hell do you leave a place like Lindenwood and walk right back into it, into another place filled with an alleged past that surpasses horror in its most terrifying form? It makes no sense. No sense at all.*

She stood and started for the phone. She must call Meda now. As she picked up the receiver to dial Meda's number, she heard a guttural, scratchy voice call out. The terrifying tone was piercing to her ears, and Natalie dropped to her knees in horror. It had clearly screamed the name "Anna".

CHAPTER 12

Natalie had spent the last several hours in a panic-stricken stupor as she struggled to come to grips with the day's events. Hearing the entity scream her daughter's name had unnerved her and left her mind spinning in a frightened abyss. After getting Anna and Timothy settled for the night, she collapsed in her bed. Sleep crept upon her.

Natalie's sleep was busy and restless. Visions of Henry Lynch darkened her dreams. She saw him towering over an open grave looking down at a body lying lifeless in the freshly dug earth. It was the body of a dead girl, presumably his daughter. Her face was partially covered by the dirt as he began filling the grave with his shovel. Her pale white dress was now soiled and wrinkled.

As Natalie stood silently watching in her lucid state, she witnessed a dark shadow moving slowly across the lot. The shadowy form circled the grave hovering a few feet above Henry Lynch's head. He was unaware of its presence. He was being stalked by something he had no defense against, but its intentions were evident. It wanted to take Henry Lynch.

Natalie gasped, breathing fast as the vision intensified. Her sheets were soaked with sweat as she viewed a horrific past event. She was seeing what really happened the day that Henry Lynch died.

The shadow loomed over Henry's back waiting to confront him. Henry placed the velvet pouch against his daughter's chest and stood up to climb out of the grave. Suddenly, he felt an ice cold gust of wind sweep over him. He stood frigid, his skin tingling, as prickles of fear covered the length of his body. Something was there, something sinister. Then, with a violent force, it came upon Henry Lynch. It showed its face as it growled at him. It was the face of pure evil. Destruction. Despair. Its eyes glowed from the depths of two black hollow holes. Its skin was mangled with rotten channels of veins oozing a foul, black secretion. The vile sounds escaping its disfigured mouth caused Henry Lynch's heart to pound heavily inside his chest. He gasped for breath, trembling as he cowered down into the grave. As the malevolent spirit towered over Henry at the edge of the grave, he raised his hand to cover his eyes in an effort to shield them from the terror that was determined to take him. Henry Lynch panted as his heart exploded. The last sensation that Henry Lynch felt was his own body hitting the earth beneath him.

Natalie jolted awake. Tears streaming down her face, she surveyed the room and realized that she was in her own bed. She concluded that she must have been dreaming. Or, was she? She threw her legs over the side of the bed and started for the door.

Thousands of thoughts marched through her mind. She had gotten some answers, some clues about Henry Lynch the day before. Maybe that's what had caused her frightening dream. Or was someone trying to communicate with her? She didn't know that Timothy had been playing with the Ouija board just days before. But it wouldn't have mattered. Natalie Houston wouldn't have understood the severity of what was happening during the game.

Natalie spent the following day researching Henry Lynch's family lineage. It was almost impossible to find anything about him because of the time period. Either very little information was recorded, or it was not preserved prior to the late 1800's.

Natalie sat in the hard, wooden chair surrounded by multiple books that she had stacked on the table in front of her. She flipped through the pages searching for any clues into Henry Lynch's past when suddenly a name caught her eye. She stared at the book and slid her finger across the page as she examined the entry. There in plain, black ink was the name Annie Mae Lynch.

Natalie gasped. Her fingers slid off the page as she slumped back in the chair. Henry Lynch's daughter was named Annie, the same seven year old daughter that he had buried in his yard. The one he had supposedly killed after losing his mind. How could all this be happening? It was too coincidental. It was madness.

She gathered her things and headed home. As she turned down the road leading to her house, she felt compelled to follow it to the cabin. The road twisted around to a dead end where Ruth Madison lived. Natalie parked the car on the side of the yard and walked to the west corner. She examined a pile of timber that had been left to rot since the cabin's construction. Was this where Annie Mae Lynch had been buried? Natalie had the strange sensation that she was being watched. She sensed a presence in her midst and felt compelled to leave. She was fast to move across the yard not bothering to look behind her as her feet shuffled through the knee high grass. Her curiosity and desire to enter the cabin had quickly diminished. From where she stood, she saw no trace of a grave. But as she turned to walk back to her car, she distinctly heard the voice of a little girl calling out "Mommy".

CHAPTER 13

Nightfall shadowed the small, brick home as Natalie prepared for bed. She had not mentioned her recent discoveries to anybody, and she felt more vulnerable for it. She was too busy processing the information and hoping that her fears would magically disappear. She was not prepared to deal with anymore hauntings or even the idea of it, but Lindenwood had only been an introduction.

In the next room, Anna Houston snuggled deep beneath the covers. She closed her eyes and yawned as sleep began to overtake her. The house was now quiet. The only audible noise was the occasional settling of the rafters, the typical clicks and pops.

Her breath became a cold, damp fog as the temperature dropped. She stirred and whimpered beneath the covers. Then the footsteps came. The thumping was loud and now at her room as the door slowly swung open. It stood watching her. It began circling her bed, swirling around the room with a strange curiousness.

Anna jerked awake. The chilling temperature lingered for a moment as she stared into the darkness. She struggled to breathe as fear gripped her. Someone was in the room with her. She knew it. She gulped for air as she felt her body being consumed by an invisible force. Anna seemed possessed as she felt her own hand rising in the air, turning to grab her face. She began whispering prayers as tears streamed from her eyes. What was happening to her? Was it just a bad dream?

She wrestled away from the bed and attempted to run for the light switch. As she turned the corner of the bed, a loud crash startled her. Glass splintered across the room. She lunged forward reaching for the switch. As the light illuminated the room, she gasped upon realizing that the sound of shattering glass once belonged to her prized porcelain collection. It had mysteriously flown off the bookcase and crashed to the floor.

She scooped up what she could of the remaining pieces and wandered down the hall. The sound of the wall clock ticking in the background caused Anna to glance toward the kitchen door. A shadowy figure caught her eye. It moved slowly forward floating across the floor. There was no face, but she could see a distinct human shape as it began to fade before her. She cried out and rushed backward into the hall. She pushed open Natalie's door and climbed into the bed where her mother lay sleeping, oblivious to anything going on around her. Anna buried her face into the extra pillow and tried to wait until sunlight.

Anna woke as Natalie began to stir. Natalie turned and noticed her lying next to her.

"Anna? When did you get in bed with me? Are you okay, honey?" Natalie wondered what had caused her daughter to abandon her own room. In the past, Anna rarely left her own bed.

Anna stretched and rolled over. "I'm scared, Mama. I don't want to go back in there. Something was in my room last night. It broke my porcelain collection, and then I saw it in the kitchen."

Chills ran up the back of Natalie's neck. "What do you mean? What did you see?"

"I don't know what it was. It looked like the shadow of a man, Mama. It scared me so bad. It was swirling around my bed. It pushed my door open and came in."

Natalie froze, unable to speak. She finally managed to wrap her arms around Anna, holding her as she rubbed her hair. "I am so sorry, honey.

Maybe it was just a bad dream." Natalie didn't know how to tell her children that she was also scared. And she was mad. Hadn't she and her children been through enough already? She wondered when peace would be restored to their lives.

Anna sobbed. "No, Mama. It wasn't a dream. It was real. It was very real. I even felt it holding my arms in my bed. I thought it was going to choke me. It was so dark. I couldn't see, but I felt it. I really did. And when I tried to jump out of bed, it pushed my collection off the bookshelf. Did the ghost from Lindenwood follow us?"

"No, no, Honey. No ghost followed us. Don't worry." Natalie's tone was reassuring, but her own doubt lingered just beneath the surface.

Natalie helped Anna to her room. As she entered the doorway, she came to an abrupt stop. She stared at the floor where the remaining splinters of glass lay scattered. She surveyed the remains with a sense of sadness. She had enjoyed collecting the miniature dolls and what-not items for Anna since her birth. Now nothing was left but the remnants of memories.

Natalie became enraged. She screamed out at the invisible force that had made a playhouse out of her new home. "Who are you? What do you want? This is my house, damn you!"

A dead silence filled the air. Anna clung tightly to her mother's side, afraid that the shadow would surely return now.

"Get out of my house! Do you hear me? I said, GET OUT!" Natalie's rage echoed throughout the house, waking Timothy.

Then without warning, the voiceless entity unleashed a violent force unlike anything they had witnessed thus far. The kitchen cabinet doors slammed open and shut with a resounding force. The earsplitting bangs consumed the entire house. Natalie and Anna screamed, covering their ears as they raced out of the room and into the kitchen.

Natalie fell to her knees with horror as she witnessed the cabinets swinging violently back and forth. Anna cried and raced to Timothy's bedroom. As she flung the door open, he sped past her and down the hall to his mother's side. His mouth hung open upon finding the source of all the noise.

"What the hell is going on?" Timothy yelled.

"Get your sister! Let's get out of here!" Natalie screamed.

"Anna, come on!" Timothy called out to her and ran back to his room where he found her hiding behind his door. He grabbed her and followed Natalie as she raced out the back door. The Oldsmobile slung tiny shards of gravel into the air as they fled.

CHAPTER 14

Natalie sped out of the subdivision. Nobody spoke as they all stared ahead in shock. Natalie had to think. She pulled off to the side of the road and placed the car in park. She turned around to face Timothy and Anna.

Natalie breathed a sigh of relief. "I think everybody is ok now."

"Mom, what are we going to do?" Timothy leaned forward resting his arm on the back of the seat.

"I don't know yet. I just don't know. "

"Mama, I don't want to go back there", Anna pleaded.

Natalie shook her head as she rubbed her fingers across her mouth. She refused to leave this house. It was hers. She had no choice to leave Lindenwood. Devon was deranged and dangerous, but this house belonged to her and her children. Nothing and nobody was going to force her to leave a place for which she had worked so hard. One way or another, she would rid the property of this spirit, of its negative energy.

She now understood that her problems couldn't be solved through ordinary means. Her problems were of a supernatural nature. Something she had never really believed in.

Natalie looked at Anna. She reached for Anna's hand and held it in hers. "You don't worry, Honey. This is our house. And, nothing is going to force us to leave it. Whatever it is, we will send it away to never bother us again."

"But, how? How can we get rid of it?"

"I have a friend who may be able to help us."

"Mom, is our house really haunted?" Timothy chewed his bottom lip as he thought of the Ouija board that he had used a few days before. He was now scared that he might have caused all this trouble by summoning the spirits.

"I don't know, Tim. But I do know that something is not right. I haven't told anybody except Meda, but I have been trying to find out the history of our home. You know that cabin? The cabin across from us?"

Timothy nodded. "Yeah, Anna and I went over there one day. It's cool."

Natalie hesitated. "Wait. What?"

"Yeah, we went over there. It's just an old cabin, Mom."

"I don't want you two playing over there anymore. Do you understand me?" Natalie gave Timothy a stern look.

"Yes, ma'am. Ok. But, Mom, why?"

"The neighbor up the street said that there are graves over there. You don't have any business wandering around that place."

"You must have talked to Mr. Jack. He told me all about it." Timothy informed her.

"Oh, he did? Natalie looked at Timothy with raised eyebrows.

"Yes, he did."

"Did Mr. Jack tell you anything about the people who used to live there or how they died?"

Timothy became worried as he noticed his mother's frown and the displeasure in her voice. "No, not really. I-I don't remember. He just said that I probably shouldn't go over there."

"Timothy, Mr. Jack told me that a man named Henry Lynch lived there in the 1800's. He also told me that the old man went crazy and killed his family. I don't know if any of that part is true, but I do know that Henry Lynch lived there. And, he had a young daughter named Anna."

Timothy and Anna gasped simultaneously. Anna, spooked by this new information, began to cry.

Natalie nodded. "And she is supposedly buried over there in the West corner. Now, I am not sure about this. Maybe it is all just a coincidence, but I am wondering if the spirit of Henry Lynch is responsible for what's been happening to us."

"What can we do?" Anna had stopped crying and now listened with curiosity.

"I am going to talk to Meda. She can help."

"Can she talk to the spirits?" Timothy asked.

"We will find out." Natalie offered.

"Mom, I think I need to tell you something."

"What? What's wrong?"

"Have you ever heard of a Ouija board?"

"Yes. Why?"

"I am afraid that I caused all this. It's supposed to just be a game, but something happened one night when I was using it."

"You were using the Ouija board in our house? In our new house? When?"

"A few days ago, Mom. But, I didn't know it was going to cause all this trouble."

Natalie was agitated. "Who was playing with you? Anna?"

Anna began shaking her head. "No, Anna wasn't with me. I was alone." Timothy explained.

Natalie placed both hands over her face as the reality sank in. She rubbed her eyes and kept her thoughts to herself. Then without another word, she put the car in drive and headed straight to Meda's.

✝

CHAPTER 15

The next morning, Natalie made plans to accompany Meda to a nearby community where she promised help would be waiting. With Timothy and Anna safe at school, the two women headed out to meet Clara Higgs. Meda had known Clara for many years. She was a very spiritual woman with supernatural gifts that were unknown to many. Clara's secrets were safely guarded. She didn't need small town folks finding out that she communicated with the dead. Stories such as that, if they got around, could get her excommunicated from the town.

Meda gave Natalie directions as the car winded through a secluded rural area. She motioned for her to turn left at the next gravel road. Natalie looked ahead to see a small-framed house surrounded by oak trees. She drove to the end of the drive and parked near the front steps.

As she and Meda got out of the car, Clara Higgs limped out the door and onto the porch, where she braced herself on a nearby column. She was a fragile woman near eighty years of age. Severe arthritis had caused her much pain over the last two years leading to her inability to put any weight on her right leg. Sometimes she relied on a cane.

Her hair was waist length and laced with gray strands among what was once her dark brunette tresses. Her eyes were a rich brown full of compassion and kindness. Her olive complexion showed sun damage. She wore a long, denim dress decorated with jewelry that was inspired by the Native American culture.

Hi, Clara." Meda was eager to embrace Clara.

"It's so good to see you. And this is your friend, Natalie?" Clara extended her hand to Natalie.

"It's very nice to meet you, Clara." Natalie was already fascinated by Clara and by her strong aura. Her eyes conveyed love and understanding as she stared back at Natalie.

"You ladies come inside and sit down. Let's talk about how I can help you, Natalie." Clara motioned for the front door, and the women walked in.

Natalie felt a tremendous release as her fear and worry began to subside. She had come to the right place. She could feel it. She saw it in Clara's eyes. There was something very special about the woman, and it was unlike anything she had experienced before. She had met other spiritual people during her lifetime. She had been raised by and among ministers of the faith, but today she had looked into the eyes of someone whom she knew had mysterious gifts; gifts that must not be shared without careful discernment.

Clara motioned for Natalie to sit across from her. "Meda tells me that you have quite a story to tell after living at Lindenwood."

Natalie looked at Meda who gave her an approving nod. "Yes, it was very traumatizing for me and my children. We were only there a few months, but I didn't think that I was going to get out of there alive."

Clara leaned back in her chair. "Natalie, I want you to tell me about what's happening where you live. I need to know everything."

Natalie shifted in to a more comfortable position and began to disclose the past four weeks' events. Clara listened intently, her hands folded in her lap. She nodded often as Natalie recounted her and her children's experiences of mysterious footsteps, objects flying across the room, and shadow figures appearing out of nowhere. But when Natalie began to discuss the history of Henry Lynch, Clara Higgs moved to the edge of her chair and leaned forward as if she didn't want to miss a single word.

"I found out that the man who lived in the cabin was a man named Henry Lynch. There is a story that tells of his going insane and killing his family. I wasn't able to find out who owned the property before him. The courthouse documents stated that he had purchased one hundred seventy-one acres from the United States of America." Natalie paused as she waited for Clara's response.

"When? What year did he purchase the property?"

"It was 1838." Natalie felt a chill and rubbed her arms.

Clara was silent for a moment as she studied Natalie's face.

"I'm going to send you home with some sage sticks and directions on what I want you to do. I want you to make peace with this spirit. Tell it that you mean it no harm, but tell it that you and your children intend to stay in your home. Tell it that you are not leaving and you wish to live there peaceably. Light the end of this sage stick and wave it in every corner of every room in your home. Ask God to bless the house and rid it of any negative energy that may be lingering there." Clara handed Natalie two four-inch sage sticks wrapped tightly together with red string. Natalie put the sticks close to her nose as she inhaled the aroma.

"Thank you, Clara." Natalie managed. Clara smiled.

"Now, Natalie. There will be a slight odor, but it shouldn't be too bad. I want you to try this first and let me know if things improve in your home."

"What is this supposed to do?" Natalie examined the sticks, curious about their proclaimed ability to ward off spirits.

"It is believed that burning sage expels negative energy. It is an ancient practice that has been used for centuries; and for good reason, it works." Clara stood up from her chair.

"I want you to call me in two days and let me know if this helps. I am hoping that your problems are a simple fix."

"What do you mean?"

Clara sighed. "If this doesn't help, we will have to explore another option. It will require outside help beyond what I can do. I will need to communicate with the spirits and try to persuade them to move on."

Natalie eyes were wide. "You would need help?"

"Yes, there are three other people that I can contact to assist me. But, first try this."

Natalie nodded. "I will. Clara, I don't want to go through this anymore. I just want my home to feel safe. My kids deserve peace."

Clara patted Natalie's arm. "Do not worry, Dear. Just do as I say."

Natalie and Meda picked up their purses and made their way to the front door. Clara followed close behind them onto the front porch and watched as the women walked to the car.

Suddenly Natalie realized something and turned to look at Clara. She took a breath before speaking, hesitating for just a moment. "Clara?"

"Yes, Dear?"

"You said that you can communicate with the dead?"

"Yes, I can."

Natalie was intrigued. "Can you talk to Henry Lynch?" Natalie wasn't prepared for what Clara was about to say.

"No, Dear, I can't."

"Oh." Natalie dropped her head with disappointment. She turned to open the car door.

Clara cleared her throat. "I can't speak to Mr. Lynch because he won't let me. He hasn't stopped chattering since you walked through the door."

Natalie's mouth fell open and she jerked around to meet eyes with Clara. Her skin tingled. Clara nodded and waved goodbye. She turned to walk back in the house and was overcome with fear at the sound of Henry Lynch's pleas.

Clara grabbed her ears as if to shield them from a loud noise. But the noises weren't audible. They were coming by telepathic means, and Henry Lynch wanted to be sure that someone could hear him as he shouted incessantly from the other side.

CHAPTER 16

Natalie spent the next two days reading everything that she could find on the subject of the paranormal and hauntings. She wanted to know what she was dealing with since her recent experiences no longer gave her the option of disbelieving. She was compelled to believe in something she had never before accepted as possible.

She had cleansed her home as Clara had instructed her to do, and she was amazed at the miraculous change in the atmosphere. Considering all of the recent happenings, it was an indescribable peace that had descended over the home immediately following the ritual. She was satisfied and had hope that the haunting was now over, but she continued in her research, as it reassured her, and it prepared her for a possible reoccurrence. Even so, what she didn't realize was that she had become a conduit, attracting the same negative entity that had terrorized Henry Lynch over a hundred years before.

One week earlier, Clara Higgs had put to rest Natalie's haunting and most of her fears along with it. And after Natalie called her and told her of the tranquility that now described the state of her home, she had no further reason for concern. Except that Henry Lynch had not stopped communicating with her. He was relentlessly invading her sleep and pleading to be heard. Her attempts to block him from accessing her mind had proven futile. He had entered Natalie's home through her mind, using her fear as energy to persist.

It was a week since Natalie had cleansed her home. Clara prepared for bed and locked all the interior doors. She turned the television off and made her way down the dimly lit hallway. She entered her bedroom, left her slippers by the door, and slid underneath the covers. There was an eerie and almost heavy silence in the room. She struggled to close her eyes and force sleep. She knew something was lurking nearby but she tried desperately to block it out of her mind as she called on the name of the archangel, Michael.

"Michael, Archangel of God, defend me against the forces of evil." Suddenly Clara's bed began to vibrate until it shook violently. The wooden legs of the bed thumped on the floor. Clara screamed out as she tried to slide off the edge of the bed.

"In the name of Jesus Christ, I command you to leave this house and to never return." Clara shouted at the invisible entity.

Pictures began to fly across the room, hurdling themselves at her. She kneeled down on the floor and continued to pray as the entity became even more incensed. It formed a dark cloud moving across the wall and onto the ceiling. Clara looked up and screamed when she saw its face, the same face and the same black hollow eyes that had stopped Henry Lynch's heart. It suspended itself hanging like a bat as it glared down into her eyes.

Clara reached for her Bible and began quoting passages. As the entity eyed her from the ceiling, she sat still as she shouted Isaiah 41:10. "Do not fear, for I am your God. I will strengthen you and help you; I will uphold you with my righteous right hand."

Clara continued to chant the name of Jesus as she envisioned a massive white light surrounding her. It was the light of God and she was calling it. Her body began to tingle, and she felt the heaviness subsiding in the room. The entity began to growl and screech as it dissipated. The bed ceased shaking.

Clara let out a heavy sigh of relief and slowly got to her feet. She turned on the bedside lamp and leaned against the bedpost. She rubbed her face and wiped away the tears that had pooled down her cheeks. She knew what was happening now. There was more to Natalie's story than she had been told.

Natalie had not only exposed Clara to Henry Lynch, but also to a demonic battle, one for which Clara was not physically equipped.

She reached for the phone on the bedside table. She dialed Meda and waited as the phone's unanswered rings pulsated in her ears. Finally, Meda picked up.

"Meda. This is Clara." She was breathless.

"What's wrong, Clara?" Meda asked. "You sound scared."

"I'm ok, but yes, I had a terrible scare tonight, just a few minutes ago."

"Wh-What happened?" Meda was worried. Clara was almost eighty years old and not in the best health.

"I need you to call Natalie and check on them. I don't think that cleansing is going to work after just that one time."

"Why? What do you mean? What is going on?" Meda was suddenly panicked.

"Natalie is being haunted by the man she talked about last week. Henry Lynch. But, something worse is going on, something much worse."

"What? What the hell is happening?"

"There is demonic activity following that family, plaguing their peace. And, I just saw it. It was here in my house a few minutes ago. Whatever this is, it knows that I am capable of helping Natalie and it wants to make sure that I don't."

"Oh my God, Clara. Are you going to be okay?"

"I will be fine. Everything is okay now. But do what I said. And tell Natalie that we must act quickly. We have no time left. I will get my people together, and we will be at her house by the weekend. Tell her to keep an eye on her children, a very close, watchful eye. It may try to harm them."

Meda's hands began to shake. Her voice was trembling. "I will call Natalie now."

"Good, I will see you in a few days."

Meda sat with the receiver still to her ear and in stunned silence as she heard Clara hang up the phone. She was terrified. She was the only person in whom Natalie could confide. Natalie had chosen not to tell her mother, Sarah Cooper, about her circumstances. She wanted to handle this on her own. There was no Devon Bradford to run from anymore. There was no Lindenwood or spirits of deceased wives to fear. She had escaped, but Meda knew something was still amiss with her friend. Natalie had a way of hiding things from the world. She harbored feelings of defeat and drowned in depression on a regular basis. She might have been able to deceive the world, but she could not fool Meda. Meda knew that Natalie Houston was still very much Natalie Bradford. She was dragging her broken dreams like a chain strapped around her ankles. And it would ultimately destroy her. Now after everything she had come through, she was being victimized by another negative entity, and in her own home. Was she a magnet drawing the phenomena to her, or was it something more powerful beyond her control? The truth would soon come to light. Yes, Hell, Part II was coming.

CHAPTER 17

Meda picked up the phone and dialed Natalie's house. It was late Monday afternoon, and Natalie was putting the laundry away while Anna and Timothy concentrated on their school work. The last few days had been peaceful without any paranormal activity in their home. Upon hearing the phone ring, she turned away from the washer and answered the phone.

"Hello?" Natalie rested the phone between her ear and her shoulder as she folded a towel.

"Natalie, I need to talk to you." Meda's voice was shaky, her message urgent.

"Hey, Meda. Is everything ok?"

"I don't think so. Clara called me. Something really bad happened to her last night, and she wants to move forward with a formal cleansing this weekend."

"Uh, ok, b-but I did what she asked me to do. I did a cleansing just like she instructed me to do." Natalie's tone was more of a question than a statement.

"It must not have worked. Clara is being tormented now. She believes you have more than Henry Lynch to be worried about." Meda's fear was evident in her voice.

"My God, sure, when?" Natalie had a frightened look on her face as she stopped folding clothes and gripped the phone firmly in her hand.

"Let's plan for Saturday." Meda advised. "We will be there in the afternoon."

"What happened to Clara, Meda? What's going on? I thought everything was ok. It's been quiet around here for several days and-"

"Natalie, Clara was visited by a-"

The phone line began to crackle and pop. A low hissing noise filled the microphone and turned into a deep, sadistic growl. It screeched louder, piercing Natalie's eardrum. She dropped the receiver and grabbed her ear. She attempted to rub the pain away as she bent down to pick up the phone.

"Meda?"

The phone line was dead. Natalie breathed faster, her nerves on edge. Her hands shook as she hung up the receiver. Just as she turned away, the phone's loud ring startled her, and she jumped. She stared at the phone for a moment, shaken and nervous for whom or what might be on the other end, before answering it.

She slowly raised the receiver to her ear. "Yes, hello?" Natalie was cautious.

"Mama? Mama, it's me. I need you. Please help me."

Natalie slid down against the wall until she was sitting on the floor. Her mouth hung open in shock. She immediately recognized the voice.

"What's wrong? What do you mean? Where is your father?"

"He left me. I am all alone here. I don't have any food, and it's cold. Please. Can you come get me?"

Natalie shook her head in disbelief. She was frightened and numb. How could this be?

"What do you mean he left you? Where is he?"

"I haven't seen him or any of the others in several weeks. Dad left months ago. He moved away with Suzanne."

Natalie was quiet. Several seconds passed.

"Mama? Are you there?"

Natalie sighed. "Yes, I am here."

"Please help me. I don't have anywhere to go, and I am hungry."

Tears began to fill Natalie's eyes. "Ok, I will be there in a few minutes. You are alone?"

"Yes, no one is here. The place is a wreck."

"Ok, be ready when I pull up. You know how I feel about that place."

"Yes, I know. Thank you, Mama. Thank you so much."

Natalie hung up the phone and stood frozen. She was stunned as she continued leaning against the wall. Was this a nightmare? She had not been back to Lindenwood since she had left that place months before, and she had vowed to never return for any reason. And now, the one person who clung to her during that time was asking for help. How could a young teenage girl be abandoned by her father, and was it safe to bring her here? This would force Natalie to have to communicate with Devon.

"Kids, get in the car. We have to go." Natalie issued a loud call through the house.

"What's wrong? Mama, what's going on? Where are we going?" Anna and Timothy chimed together.

"We have to go get Audrey at Lindenwood. She is alone without food."

"What? Mama, please tell me you're not serious." Timothy studied Natalie's face.

Natalie nodded and took a deep breath. She motioned for the door. "Timothy, we are going to Lindenwood."

CHAPTER 18

Audrey Bradford stood near the front windows of the mansion. Her eyes roamed the nearby highway every few minutes in search of Natalie's blue Oldsmobile. She had packed three mismatched suitcases that she found in her father's closet. Every piece of clothing she had was neatly folded and packed. She wasn't planning on returning to Lindenwood. The mansion had been deserted. Lindenwood was home only to the memory of Liz and Caroline Bradford.

Audrey sat on the bottom step of the staircase and allowed her eyes to study each corner of the mansion as she reminisced about the days her mother walked on the very floors beneath her feet. The quietness of the house was eerie. She felt the presence of her mother and realized her mother's spirit might never rest. There was no doubt in her mind that Liz and Caroline Bradford would remain at Lindenwood long after she was gone, and that thought brought her peace, in a way in which she could feel eternally connected to her mother. She yearned for a mother in her life, and since her father's abandonment, the wounds of her mother's death had been reopened, bleeding out the agony she felt almost daily.

No one spoke as Natalie drove the thirty minute distance to Lindenwood. She knew what Anna and Timothy were thinking. No one wanted to have to re-enter that place. No one wanted to face the memories. It had been a terrifying reality only months before.

As the car winded around the rural county roads, Natalie grimaced and felt a chill upon seeing the sight of Liz and Caroline Bradford's grave across from the mansion. The two grave stones rested atop the hillside, glaring down on the house. She thought of the many times that she had looked out the second floor window only to see a mysterious, lingering mist hovering above them. She could recall feeling that they were watching her just the same.

Natalie slowed the car and turned into the driveway. The tall grass and thick weeds that bordered the beds of the front steps to the mansion made it apparent that Lindenwood had, in fact, been neglected.

"Kids, y'all can stay in the car if you want. I am going in to get Audrey." Natalie parked the car near the front of the house.

"I'm staying here, Mom." Timothy declared with a firm tone.

"Anna?" Natalie waited.

"I'm going with you." Anna looked at Natalie as if she was waiting for her approval.

"Ok, we won't be long, Tim."

Anna and Natalie walked up to the front door and opened it slowly. The house was pitch, black throughout except for a couple of candles that Audrey had lit inside. Clothes were scattered about the living room floor, and a heavy smell of trash and mildew filled the air.

"Audrey?" Natalie called out as she stepped further inside the house and stood near the entrance to the master bedroom.

The bedroom door creaked open. Natalie's body tensed as Anna stepped closer and held tighter to her. Both of them seemed to hold their breath together. Then Audrey slowly exited the room. Natalie let out a long sigh as she reached out to embrace her former stepdaughter.

"Are you okay?" Natalie hugged her and patted her back.

"I will be. I was so scared. The electric company came today and turned the power off."

Natalie shook her head in disgust. Her heart broke for Audrey. She wasn't prepared to take on someone else's child, but she couldn't refuse to help her either. She wiped away the tears that had started to run from Audrey's eyes. Natalie cleared her throat.

"Get your things, and let's get out of here, Honey."

"Ok, here. Take this extra flashlight. I need to go upstairs and get some things out of my room." Audrey started for the stairs with Natalie and Anna following close behind. The two flashlight beams danced and lit the upstairs hallway.

"Hurry, please. I don't like being in here." The house was musty and warm, and Natalie began to sweat.

She cringed as she started to walk up the stairs. She smelled the familiar scents of Lindenwood as she turned the corner of the stair rail. She moved the flashlight beam across the house, lighting up areas of the abandoned rooms as she made her way around the top floor.

Natalie was curious in spite of her fear. She wandered through the area like a soldier commemorating his final days of battle. A dark emptiness seeped down the walls of the mansion like the thick tears that must have stained Liz Bradford's face the night she died.

As Natalie continued to Audrey's room, she began to cough, and her nose burned with irritation. She covered her mouth as the stench of mildew filled her nostrils. She moved the light all around and gasped at the sight of busted tiles and insulation hanging in shreds. Splotches of brown water stains and white mold littered the pale blue carpet.

"My God, what happened here?" Natalie shouted to Audrey.

Audrey stood in the doorway carrying a suitcase in each hand. "The water pipes busted. It got too cold, and I didn't have any heat."

Natalie's eyes grew wide. "You didn't have any heat?"

Audrey shook her head.

Natalie sighed in disgust. "I'll get those suitcases. Let's get the hell out of here."

"Wait. I want to show you where my room caught fire." Audrey led Natalie through the doorway into her room.

"How did your room catch fire, Audrey?" Natalie asked in astonishment.

"I tried to burn down the house, but it wouldn't burn. I even poured gasoline on the carpet, and the flame still went out." Audrey stepped forward and patted the charred carpet with her shoe.

Natalie stared with disbelief at the five-foot wide area of scorched carpet and ashes. Anna's eyes roamed up the wall, gawking at the imprint of smoke and flames.

"Why would you want to burn down your house, Audrey?" Anna's tone was scolding.

"I hate it here. But, it wouldn't burn. Mama caused the flame to go out." Audrey spoke with assuredness. She knew her mother's spirit filled the mansion, and she remembered hearing how much her mother had loved Lindenwood.

"Let's get out of here. I never liked this place, and I sure don't like it now." Anna began to back out of the room.

Suddenly, the sound of nearby footsteps grabbed their attention. It was time to leave Lindenwood. Audrey carried an 8 x 10 picture of her mother close to her chest.

"Anna, can I put this picture up in your room while I'm staying with you?" She showed Anna the smiling face of a youthful and lively Liz Bradford.

Anna stared at the picture, hesitated, and then stopped on the stairs as she was overcome with a transcendental knowing that she hadn't experienced before now. Her hand flew to her mouth. Her eyes were tearing up and filled with fear. It was as if someone had lifted a veil from her face.

"Oh my God!" Anna whispered between her fingers.

Audrey stared at Anna with concern. Her face had grown pale. "What? What's wrong?"

"Audrey, do you believe that Lindenwood is really haunted?" Anna knew the answer, but she wanted to hear Audrey say it.

Audrey looked at Anna as if she had asked an obvious question. "Oh, yeah, definitely. Mama and Caroline are still here. I talk to Mama all the time."

Anna's skin crawled. She had never experienced the paranormal until she and her family had moved to Lindenwood. She never even knew ghosts existed until then. Even Timothy had no reason to believe in ghosts, and yet Caroline sought him out while he slept in her former room. She wondered what was happening to her and why she was experiencing strange noises and lights. What was happening to her? Didn't they leave the ghosts behind when they left Lindenwood? Or could they have followed her? It didn't make sense.

"Audrey, something followed us when we left this place." Anna spoke aloud. "But, I don't think it was your mother."

"What?" Audrey was confused. "What are you talking about, Anna?"

Anna shook her head again and pointed her finger with an air of confidence. "I know what Lindenwood has done to us, and this was only the beginning. This place opened the door to another world, the spirit world, and now spirits are trying to contact me."

Audrey's chin dropped, and her body became rigid. "You mean..."

Anna nodded quickly, interrupting Audrey. "We have our own ghost, Audrey. And I don't think it's as nice as your mama."

CHAPTER 19

Natalie phoned Devon Bradford immediately upon returning home. She tracked down his new wife, Suzanne's phone number in the telephone directory. He had to know that she had his daughter, and she had to know what to do about it.

Suzanne's phone rang incessantly as Natalie chewed her fingernails. She listened while holding her breath, fearful of hearing a "hello" on the other end.

Devon's voice was deep and devious causing Natalie to shudder. "Hello?"

Natalie paused, her heart pounding.

"Hello?" Devon listened to the silence.

"Hello. Devon?"

"Yes?"

"This is Natalie. I have Audrey."

Devon flinched. "What do you mean? You have Audrey?"

"She called me. She was living at Lindenwood all alone and with no food or heat. You know this."

Devon cleared his throat. His voice softened. "She refused to come with me. When did you get her?"

"Just a little while ago. But, I cannot keep her, Devon. When can you make arrangements to pick her up?"

The phone went silent for several seconds. "I will come get her Friday. Give me a few days. And, Natalie?"

Natalie listened and waited.

"Thank you." Devon sounded genuinely grateful which surprised Natalie.

"When will I hear from you?" Natalie asked, mentally processing the situation and astounded by this version of Devon. He seemed like a different person and not the Devon she knew.

"I will pick her up Friday at your house, by noon."

"But…but do you know where I live?" Natalie couldn't believe her ears.

"Yes, I know exactly where you live. Thanks again." Devon hung up the phone.

Natalie stood frozen against the kitchen wall. To learn of Devon knowing her new address sent a familiar shiver down her spine. Devon could be a cunning and dangerous man, but he had no reason to stalk her now. He had moved on, and she had no ties to him.

Natalie attempted to brush aside her uneasiness as she focused on the more serious problems at hand. Most important was her home that needed to be cleansed. In just a few days, Clara would be performing a ritual Natalie had never seen attempted.

Once again, Natalie felt as if she was caught in a spider's web.

In another part of the house, Audrey settled into Anna's room as they prepared for bed. She placed the 8 x 10 picture of her mother, Liz Bradford, next to the bed. Anna locked eyes with it. Liz Bradford was once a beautiful woman. Her smile made Anna feel sad as she thought about how Audrey had lost her mother. Liz's hair and makeup was reminiscent of the same style and manner by which she had been buried.

"Do you think your mama is with you all the time?" Anna turned to look at Audrey who was changing into her night clothes.

"Yes, why?" Audrey responded quickly, without any hesitation.

"I don't know. It just scares me."

"Don't be scared. She won't hurt you." Audrey wanted to assure Anna.

Anna nodded and climbed into bed. Audrey flicked off the light switch and slid onto the opposite side.

"Audrey?" Anna whispered in the dark.

"Yes?"

"There is something bad here. I hope it doesn't bother us tonight, but it might."

"What is it?"

"I don't know exactly. It's a bad spirit. It breaks things in my room and watches me. I hear it all the time."

Audrey's eyes widened. Her body tightened. "Did you lock the door?"

"Yes."

"Where are your dogs? Maybe we should sleep with them."

"They are in the hallway. They sleep right outside the door."

Audrey breathed deep. "Ok." She closed her eyes and waited for sleep to overcome her.

Four hours had passed. The house was dead silent except for an occasional pop or crackle. The dogs lay sleeping near the kitchen entrance.

The house seemed to darken as the entity slinked along the interior walls. It touched down on the floor leading to the hall. The dogs awoke and became alert as they issued a ferocious warning to the dark figure hovering before them. The hair on their backs stood up and their growling became more pronounced as the entity stood nearby now challenging them. The dogs began to back away, their bark becoming louder. Their snarls were a violent show of fangs communicating their readiness to devour the entity if it came any closer. As the dogs maintained their stance, the entity maneuvered itself away, as it climbed the walls leading directly to Anna's bedroom.

It passed through the door and slivered up the wall as it made its way to the ceiling where it dangled there, suspended in midair as it studied the two girls below. Its eyes rolled back and forth, darting around the room as its heavy breathing cast a low grunt.

Anna stirred. She heard the dogs growling as they scratched at her bedroom door. She slowly sat up resting on her elbows. Her heart palpitations grew stronger as she sensed that she was no longer alone and that the entity was back. She didn't dare look around. She pulled the covers closer to her face.

"Audrey. Audrey, wake up!" Anna whispered loudly. She gently elbowed Audrey.

The entity watched them intently as it spread itself across the ceiling. It extended itself until it covered most of the ceiling above Anna's bed.

Suddenly, Audrey jerked awake as she heard a low growl near her ear. The room was pitch-black except for the moonlight streaming through the bedroom window.

"Did you hear that?" Audrey rolled over toward Anna.

"Yes. Be quiet." Anna advised and could barely move. Her body was frozen in fear. Her breathing was shallow.

Audrey jumped out of the bed and reached for the bedside lamp switching it on.

The entity hovered overhead. Anna screamed blood curdling pleas as the dogs scratched and tore at the doorframe. Audrey cried out as she watched the entity sliver down and along the wall until suddenly it was right beside her.

"Don't look at it, Audrey! Don't look at its eyes!" Anna shouted.

Audrey began to cry. "No, please help me. Please, help!"

Timothy jumped from his bed and dashed across the hallway. He pushed on Anna's door forcing it to open. Natalie, now awake, rushed from her room and appeared in the doorway behind Timothy.

"What's wrong?!   What's going on, Girls?" Natalie managed, though she was exhausted and terrified.

The entity quickly dissolved leaving only a trace of its usual foul odor behind.

Anna and Audrey both sat up sobbing. "Something was in my room. It wasn't the old man this time. It was something else, Mama." Anna shook as she spoke.

Natalie was shaking as well.   How much longer could they last here? She worried that they would be forced to flee again.   And all she had wanted was peace for her family. She shook her head and pulled Anna and Audrey close; they shook and sobbed against her chest. Timothy lay across the foot of the bed as Natalie held the two girls.   They all drifted in and out of sleep as they waited for daylight to come.

CHAPTER 20

Anna hung a picture of Jesus Christ over her bed. She placed her bible on the bedside table and searched through the chest of drawers for a crucifix she had put away. She pulled it from the drawer and placed it near the bible. She wanted to feel protected from whatever it was that was haunting her.

Three days had passed since she had seen the dark shadow. Each morning she heard the rattling and banging of kitchen cabinets only to find upon entering the kitchen that everything was closed and untouched. It was maddening. Had she not heard what she thought she heard?

Meanwhile, Natalie prepared dinner as usual. A chill filled the air in the kitchen where she busied herself near the stove. She breathed in deeply, and she could see her breath as she exhaled. The dark and invisible presence seemed to pace back and forth across the cold, linoleum floors. It felt nothing other than the anger it had taken with it in death, and Natalie was an easy target as she unknowingly possessed a kind of magnetic energy to the spirit world.

Natalie turned as an unexpected swishing noise raced past her to the right. A cold blast enveloped her just as she glanced toward the dining table. A man dressed in old clothing stood stoic and stared back at her. She screamed as she fell back against the sink. The old man studied her.

"Who are you?! What do you want?!" Natalie shouted.

She watched in horror as the apparition of Henry Lynch walked through the kitchen wall and faded out of sight. She quickly turned the stove off and shouted for the kids to come with her.

They all ran out the back door and across the yard toward the cabin. The curious neighbor, Jack Adams, watched as the kids followed closely behind Natalie. He got up from his front porch resting spot and walked slowly in the same direction.

"Mama, what are you doing?" Timothy shouted to Natalie.

"Just follow me. I want to know what the hell happened over here. I want to know if Henry Lynch is still here."

"No way! I am not going."

"Then stay right there with Audrey and Anna. I'll be right back."

Timothy stood watching from a distance as Natalie entered the cabin. She screamed out to Henry Lynch.

"Are you here? Where are you? Why are you haunting me and my family? I want to know, damnit! Answer me!" Natalie's voice echoed from inside the cabin. Silence. But though Natalie could not see Henry Lynch, she could sense that he was watching.

Jack was quiet, stepping one foot at a time on the outdoor steps. He heard Natalie's screams. Natalie paced throughout the cabin going from one end to another as if she believed Henry Lynch would be waiting for her in one of the rooms. But the spirit of Henry Lynch was only one more tormented soul, as she had been at one time too. He had been tormented for eons and unable to change his circumstances even after death. Or so it had seemed to him.

Jack called out to Natalie. "Ma'am, are you alright?"

Natalie stood still and rigid. She looked around the corner of the cabin wall and saw Jack Adams standing on the front porch. She wondered how long he had been there and if he'd heard her calling out to Henry Lynch. Natalie hesitated before answering.

"Mr. Adams...No, I am not okay. Something is happening to me and my family. And, I'm here to put an end to it!"

Jack Adams shuffled his feet and looked toward the ground refusing to comment as Natalie studied him. Ideas about who Jack might actually be raced through her mind. He is an odd man, she thought. Why does he act so peculiar? She had only met him once when she questioned him about the cabin's history. And she wondered again what else he might know.

Natalie walked closer to Jack and stopped in front of him. "Mr. Adams, this may sound crazy to you, but since we moved into that house over there, we've been through nothing but hell. Something or someone is haunting us in our own home. And, I want some answers. I want this thing, whatever it is, gone."

Jack continued to stare at his feet. He scratched at his ear and shuffled his feet as he started to back away.

Natalie stepped forward and closer each time Jack took a step backward. "Mr. Adams, what is wrong? I feel like you know something that you aren't willing to tell me. Why?" Her tone was inquisitive but demanding of a response.

Jack shook his head and stuttered. "You-you don't want to an-anger these sp-spirits here."

"What spirits? What do you mean? Tell me."

Jack turned away and walked toward the front steps.

"Wait. Please, don't leave. I need your help. Don't you want to help me? You followed me over here. Why did you do that if you won't help me?"

Jack stopped and sat down on the step. He looked around as if he were searching for something that might be waiting to attack him. He took a deep breath and managed, "I will tell you."

Natalie sat down beside him and waited.

Jack studied his hands for a moment. "There was a terrible tragedy here. Do you remember what I told you several weeks ago when we were standing in my garden?"

Natalie nodded. "Yes. You told me that Henry Lynch had lost his mind and killed his family."

Jack shook his head. "That's not exactly what happened."

"Go on." Natalie waited with anticipation.

Jack paused for a few seconds. He turned and looked at Natalie. He studied her eyes for a moment. Natalie stared back and stood her ground. She was determined to find out the truth.

"Go on." Natalie pressed him again.

"Henry Lynch did lose his mind after the war. But, he didn't murder his children. His children were stricken with illness and died. He was forced to bury all of them in this yard."

"Stricken with illness? So, why did you tell me that he murdered them? I don't understand." Natalie's eyes remained fixed on Jack.

"Be-be-because Henry was haunted by something evil. Something took his life as he was standing over his daughter's grave." Jack began to fidget. He was sweating profusely now.

Natalie's skin began to crawl. "Haunted by something evil? You mean that shadow, the one that stopped his heart?"

"Yes, and we were told to never speak of it lessen we bring it back again. It came for Henry Lynch, and it took him."

"But, why? What reason did it have to attack Henry Lynch?" Natalie probed further, hoping Jack wouldn't refuse to explain.

"He was a tortured man. Angry. Depressed. Evil spirits attach themselves to people who live in darkness." Henry quickly began to stand. Natalie followed.

Timothy watched his mother walking away from the cabin. He wondered what Mr. Jack had told her. As he scanned the property, he noticed something white dash across the west side of the lot, like a flash of light. He moved quickly as he crept closer to the cabin area. He kept a safe distance but was able to openly view the west side. There floating across the back side of the cabin was a young girl. He stood amazed and still as he watched her float just above the ground. Her feet dangled in the air as if she were suspended by a wire. She danced in midair as she glided toward the back porch. Timothy struggled to find his voice as he watched the spirit of Annie Lynch easing closer and closer toward Natalie.

"Mom! Mom! Look behind you!" Timothy shouted with all his might. His voice cracked.

Natalie jerked around. She screamed and fell backwards at the sight of young Annie Lynch, stepping on Jack's foot as the two of them fought to escape. But just as Natalie started to break and run, Jack grabbed her arm.

"What the hell are you doing?!" Natalie yelled at Jack.

"Wait. Look." Jack stood frozen as the spirit began to mouth words.

He wiped his eyes in disbelief. Natalie's mouth was agape. Nothing the spirit was saying was audible to them, but they were astonished at its attempt to communicate.

Suddenly, as quickly as it had appeared, the spirit of Annie Lynch began to dissipate. The dark shadow was returning. Its growl was fierce as it surrounded Natalie and Jack. There was nowhere to run. As Natalie watched in horror, Jack Adams began to whimper, his feet slowly lifting off the ground.

✝

CHAPTER 21

Natalie grabbed Jack's hand, pulling him as she ran, desperate to get off the cabin property. Jack bolted toward his yard as Natalie burst through the back door of her house. Timothy and Anna followed, running across the yard.

Natalie panted as she dialed Clara's number. She tried to regain control of her breathing as she listened to the ringing. Clara picked up the phone as Natalie was taking a deep breath.

"Clara, we need you now. Please come quick. Now!" Natalie's voice screamed with urgency as she huffed into the phone.

"Natalie? Are you ok?" Clara quickly got up from her chair and began gathering her things.

"Right this minute, I am ok. But, I just witnessed something that I have never seen before. Over at the cabin. There is something there. Something evil. It's following us. It's in my house. Can you come now?"

"Yes, I will not be alone. I will be bringing more help. Now, I need you to listen to me."

Natalie's skin crawled. "I am listening."

"Make sure that everything is secure in the house. What-nots and things lying around could take flight. Put them away. We will be there soon."

"Please hurry! I think we need to cleanse this whole area. Not just my house." Natalie's tone resonated like warning sounds of danger.

Clara said goodbye and busied herself with collecting the items she would be using during the ritual. She phoned Meda and her accomplice, an unknown shaman who had performed many such rituals.

Meanwhile, Natalie hurried as she prepared the house. She put away dishes and removed anything that might cause an injury if it was suddenly hurdled across the room. She trembled as she examined each room of the house. If Clara was not successful, Natalie knew she would have to leave for good. Once again, she would be in a state of retreat. Escaping from something she didn't understand.

She heard the sound of a car as it pulled into the gravel drive. She rushed out the front door just as Clara was getting out. Meda reached to hug Natalie. She stood still for a moment as she embraced her. Natalie was distraught.

"Natalie, I want you to meet Dakota. He is a Sioux shaman." Clara whispered so that no one else could hear. Natalie looked at Clara with raised eyebrows. She was intrigued.

Dakota extended his hand and nodded. Natalie was mesmerized as she studied the elder gentleman standing before her. He was covered in strands of beads and feathers. His hair was laced with black and gray and tied tightly with a leather string behind his head.

Natalie felt a sense of dread as she watched Dakota and Clara start for the house. She could hear the faint sound of chatter between them as she watched them walking ahead. Clara was nodding in agreement to something Dakota was saying. She stopped and stared at Dakota as they engaged in deep conversation. What was being said? Dakota continued to point toward the cabin as they talked.

Natalie was filled with curiosity as she slowly approached the two of them. Just as she reached them, Dakota turned and began to walk toward the cabin property.

"Clara, what is Dakota saying?" Natalie's tone was extremely inquisitive.

Clara paused. "He feels the spirits. He knows who is here and why. They are speaking to both of us already. The energy is very strong here. And Henry Lynch, he has been chattering since we pulled up."

Natalie's mouth hung open. The hair on the back of her neck began to stand up. "What are they saying?"

"Henry Lynch wants his story set straight. Dakota and I need to be on the cabin property. That is where the most energy is coming from. The unrest starts there. But, there is something else. We know about the evil presence."

"How do you know? What do you mean?"

"We know it's here. And, it has held Henry Lynch's soul for more than a century."

Clara started for the cabin property. She followed a short distance behind Dakota. Natalie called out after her. "But, how do you know that it is here now?"

Clara stopped and turned to look at Natalie. "I heard it hissing your name when I got out of the car."

CHAPTER 22

Clara and Dakota began setting up the scene for a ritual cleansing. No one was allowed to enter the property after they had formed a sacred circle that enclosed the entire cabin, including the grave site of Annie Lynch. Natalie watched from a distance while Jack Adams, Timothy, Audrey, and Anna stood nearby. Meda was allowed to participate, from a distance, as a prayer warrior.

The chanting began while smoke from burning herbs trailed up into the sky and around them. At much surprise to Natalie, the spirits were calm. The entire fifteen minute cleansing was uneventful. And she wondered; had the spirits already left? In any case, it appeared as though the cleansing had been successful. The area was quiet. Even the wind in the trees only produced an occasional rustling of leaves.

Clara and Dakota began to make their way back to Natalie's house. The two of them were somber as they walked towards her with their heads down. Natalie was perplexed. What had just happened? Was it over? Was that it? Wasn't this supposed to occur during evening hours anyway?

Clara stopped in front of Natalie as Dakota began to circle Natalie's house on foot. Natalie could hear him in the distance speaking in an unknown language, chanting. He was scattering something on the ground, thoroughly, as he made his way around her property.

"Natalie, Dakota and I are now going to attempt to clear your land. At the moment, the cabin area appears to be clear. The problem wasn't there anymore. It's here in your house..."

Natalie stared at Clara wide-eyed. "I don't understand. What do you mean?"

Clara reached for Natalie's hands. And she immediately gasped as she felt Natalie's energy. She was reading Natalie; she knew her thoughts at that very moment. She knew the darkness that had masqueraded as a haunting all along. It all made sense now. Henry Lynch had revealed to her his own battle with the demon. And this demon had attached itself to another; Natalie had become a conduit for the same demon that had taken the life of Henry Lynch over one hundred years before.

Natalie squeezed Clara's hands. "What's wrong? Tell me!"

Clara struggled to catch her breath. "Natalie, Henry Lynch told me his story while Dakota and I were at the cabin. He did not kill his children. He was tormented by a dark entity after he lost everything during the Civil War. It destroyed his life. And because of his frailty, and because of his inability to overcome his sorrow, he was particularly susceptible to its ill doings. Ultimately, it caused his death. Henry Lynch has been watching your daughter because she has a porcelain doll that very much resembles the doll with which he buried Annie. His spirit is still in mourning. Angered and tormented."

"How do I fit into this?" Natalie was confused.

"You are confused, depressed, and wallowing in despair much like Henry Lynch. Your past haunts you. Not Henry, not Liz Bradford. It's you that needs cleansing, Natalie. Healing," Clara spoke firmly.

Natalie bowed her head. Tears seeped from her eyes and down her cheeks as she nodded in agreement.

"Let's go inside and get this done. There is definitely a dark energy here, but I believe we can remove it." Clara motioned for Natalie to follow.

Natalie stopped just inside the door. She turned to Clara. "I did not imagine all of this. Lindenwood was haunted. That wasn't my imagination. And here? I know what I am experiencing. I know this is real."

Clara nodded. "You are right. All of these things happened. But if you want to stop the hauntings, you have to recognize and acknowledge any fear or guilt within you. You must heal the dysfunction within you. You have become a magnet for this activity. Do you understand?"

Natalie looked away. "I think so."

"You have hid it well, Natalie. You have internalized your own grief, but you have to release the demons that you are fighting within, that are fighting for your sanity and your soul. You can't change your mistakes. But you must learn to forgive yourself and others, or it will consume you. It becomes a poison that seeps into the deepest corners of your thoughts. And dark energy feeds off of this. It revels in your doubts and fears. Don't you see?"

Natalie nodded. She followed Clara to the living room where Dakota was waiting. Clara went to stand right next to him as he began to speak blessings over the house and over Natalie. His eyes were closed as he concentrated.

The temperature in the room began to drop. A chilling breeze swirled through and around the room as the dark entity revealed itself to them. The black shadow scratched the side of the wall as it leapt onto the ceiling. Its face was dark, almost hidden, but its voice screamed obscenities while Dakota and Clara commanded it to leave.

Natalie fell backwards against the sofa as the entity wrapped itself around her. It squeezed the breath out of her body. She gasped and choked for air, her hands clawing at her throat. Meda shook with fear but continued to pray reciting the Psalms. No one could do anything to help Natalie. She had to endure the hostility of the entity, in order for the cleansing, the removal of the entity to work. It wanted to destroy her just as it had wanted to destroy Henry Lynch.

Dakota shouted louder as Natalie's hair began to rise above her head. Terrified, Natalie screamed.

She was helpless and horrified. Dakota reached out his hand and placed it on her head. He allowed his healing light to exude from his body and into Natalie's. It was working. His hands trembled as he felt that energy leaving him, and Natalie became quiet.

The entity screeched and growled, jumping onto the wall. It hung upside down, panting as it laughed and leered at all of them. The kitchen cabinets began to swing open. Loud thumps echoed throughout the house as it climbed above them. Its face was now visible to them.

"Stay focused! No one look at its face! Close your eyes if you must, but do not look at it! I call on the name of Yahweh! Fill this room with divine light! It cannot survive in the light!" Dakota shouted insistently.

Clara stepped forward. "Meda, Dakota, give me your hands!"

The three of them joined hands as they summoned Divine Light. The room began to glow, becoming brighter as their chanting continued and intensified. Beads of sweat began to seep from their skin as they relentlessly commanded the entity to leave.

Its face twisted and its mouth expelled vile black ooze as its eyes changed from a far-reaching black to a flaming red. It jumped in front of Dakota, confronting him as it continued to mock him and the others with a high-pitched diabolical laugh. Dakota refused to flinch or to back down. He refused to look into its eyes. His chants became louder, more deliberate. He summoned the light, extruding a great force of energy from his body. Beaming shards of light pulsated away from him. The entity shrieked as it started to dissolve right before everyone's eyes. The cabinet doors slammed shut as a bright calm settled over the house.

"Natalie, I see Henry Lynch. He is here. I am talking to him." Clara's eyes were still closed and scrunched, her head bowed.

"He said to tell Anna that he is sorry that he broke her porcelain collection. He didn't mean to."

Natalie's mouth hung open in awe. Tears poured down her cheeks as she listened to Clara.

"I am sending him into the light, Natalie. So that he can rest now. Oh, and he's with his daughter, Annie. They are holding hands."

Clara nodded as if Henry was physically there. "Go home, Henry."

Clara watched as a white light surrounded Henry and Annie Lynch. It was done.

Meda rushed to Natalie's side, hugging her tightly. Natalie felt an indescribable peace. Clara reached for Natalie's hand.

"It is finished." Clara reassured her. "Live in peace." She squeezed Natalie's hand.

"Are they all gone? Can they come back?" Natalie's tone was filled with doubt and uncertainty.

Clara sat down next to her, and looked Natalie in the eyes. Her facial expression was full of love and compassion. "Yes, it could. Pray to God that it doesn't."

Clara slowly began to stand. She gathered her things and started for the door. Dakota offered Clara his arm for support as he helped escort her out of the house.

Natalie wiped tears from the corners of her eyes as a sense of relief swept over her. She stood silent in the doorway as she and Meda watched Clara and Dakota drive away. Natalie had been shown what she needed to see in order to restore serenity to her life. Although she had been a victim at Lindenwood, she now realized that she possessed the power to stop the hauntings all along. As the taillights of the car faded from sight, she stepped back and closed the door. Meda reached for her hand and pulled Natalie toward her in a tight and comforting embrace.

It was the end of Natalie Bradford's haunting. And it would be the last time that Natalie ever spoke of Lindenwood. From this day forward, if anyone ever questioned Natalie about her ghostly encounters, her response was always the same and somewhat characteristic of her denial even in the face of a paranormal reality.

"There were things that happened that could not be explained." She reasoned.

The End

Have you heard about this story?

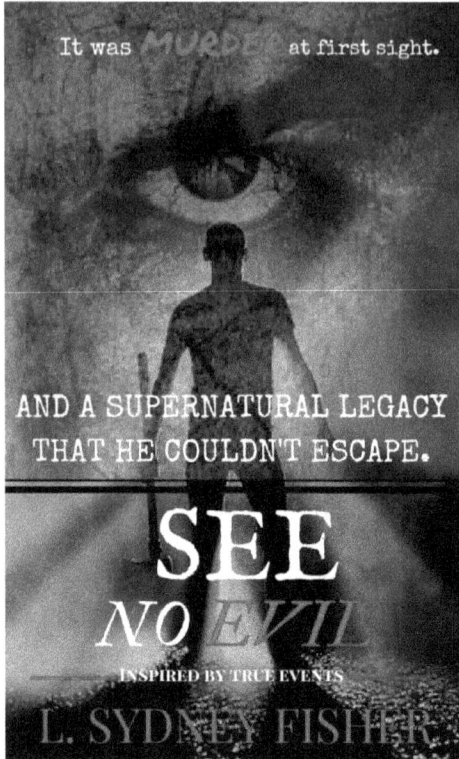

A story inspired by the real life Mississippi Mystic, Seymour Prater. Known throughout the South for his mysterious and miraculous abilities, he could "see" beyond the barriers of time and space while identifying a man's killer, finding stolen objects, and even locating lost people. Seymour Prater left behind a supernatural legacy and one unsolved murder that terrified a Mississippi town as the community battled their fears of the living and a dead man's ghost that haunted the 'Old Floyd Place'.

READING SAMPLE

Chapter 1

Missionary Ridge. Chattanooga, Tennessee
November 25, 1863
3:00 p.m.

The sound of footsteps sliding across the grassy slope alerted the Rebel forces of an impending attack as the Federals charged up the side of the mountain, their boots heavy and marred with mud formulated from the recent rain. As they pushed forward into Confederate territory, they began to shout, their roars echoing across the side of the ridge.

"Chickamauga! Chickamauga!" The Federals chanted in unison.

Confederate General Braxton Bragg stared into the face of certain victory, his deep brown eyes moistened by the chilling blast that swept over his face and caused him to step backwards. It was a warning; a cold harbinger alerting him of the end as he quickly began to order his men's retreat. But the order came too late as the federal troops advanced. The Yankees had begun to charge the ridge without the order from Union General Thomas George. They had taken the advance under their own promissory and burst forth with a force so powerful that thousands of men fell to their deaths. Haunting screams could be heard as bodies tumbled hundreds of feet down the hillside while others found their graves where they fell.

Blood splattered in every direction as bullets split skulls and severed carotid arteries. The bloody death found its mark upon the hands of some of the men still standing who, in a desperate attempt to save their best friend's life, dragged the lifeless body until their own need to survive forced them into abandonment.

Thomas Jefferson Brown, 34th Alabama Infantry Regiment, Company B, fell to his knees. He grimaced in pain as his kneecaps hit the rocky slag surface. His feet cramped inside his boots and his arms trembled from fatigue. He held his musket tight, his head lowered and his eyes closed as he felt the enemy's encirclement.

Just as the enemy's shouts rang loud, he felt a quick, hard thrust from the bottom of a boot. The Yankee kicked him breathless and sent his body forward as he slammed face first into the rock. The tender skin of his left brow split open and began to bleed, the blood trickling into his eye socket.

"Get up, Soldier. Get up and fight." The Yankee mocked him and attempted to roll his body over with his foot.

Thomas Jefferson Brown was not near death, but he might as well been. He was now a captured Confederate soldier and a prisoner of war to the

Federals. Seconds seemed like hours as his mind played back the conversation that he had with his best friend, Lewis Meadow Prater who was serving with him. Both men had enlisted in Coosa County, Alabama. The regiment was organized April 15, 1862 and then moved to Tupelo, Mississippi and placed under General Arthur M. Manigault's Brigade.

Prater and Brown had it made in Tupelo. The camp was well-guarded and food was plentiful. They were positioned on the east side in a Confederate camp that housed several hundred men overlooking the city. It was on this hillside where Prater and Brown ate their evening supper of corn, salt pork, and bread while sitting around the glowing campfires that could be seen almost a mile away near General Bragg's headquarters. The Tupelo camps were a part of what became known as the "Black Prairie" because of its fertile land. Crops were easily grown in abundance and livestock was plentiful. Thus, Tupelo and its region were capable of feeding the entire Confederate Army of the West.

On the evening before Prater and Brown were set to depart for Chattanooga, Brown unknowingly revealed a man's destiny. During the evening meal, he nudged his friend, Lewis Prater while both men finished the last of their bread rations.

"Lewis, my good friend, I have an urgent request of you and beg for your consent." Thomas Jefferson Brown locked eyes with his closest friend as he thought of his wife back in Coosa County, Alabama. What would happen to Martha if she became a widow? How would she raise their two sons alone? Prater was his first consideration. Although Prater was nineteen years old, he had never married and had no children.

Prater looked intently at Brown as he broke a piece of bread. "Yes, of course. What is it?"

Brown looked away and hesitated for a brief moment as he collected his thoughts then glanced back at Prater. "I need you to promise to take care of Martha if I'm killed. I need you to promise me that you'll do it. Please. She'll be raising my sons alone. You aren't married, and it would be an honor to me."

Prater's eyes moistened as he stared into the eyes of his best friend and considered the reality that one of them might be killed within a few days. Would this be the last meal that he had with his best friend?

Prater accepted the bread that Brown passed to him. The reality of war was upon them. "I'm honored by your request. I pray that we both come home, but I will promise to take care of your family if something happens to you. You have my word." Prater stood up and Brown joined him in front of the campfire as the two men embraced. Tears moistened the eyes of the best friends. Then Brown pulled back and looked Prater in the eyes. His hands were now clasped together as if he was about to pray. "Thank you. Thank you, my friend."

Brown's mind quickly snapped back to the present as he felt his hands being bound with a leather strap. The leather stung as it was tightened around his wrists almost cutting off the circulation. Two men hoisted him to his feet and shoved him forward forcing him to walk down the hill where he would join over 5,000 other Confederates now destined for Rock Island, Illinois.

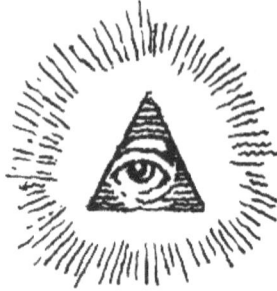

Chapter 2

Thomas Jefferson Brown climbed into the railcar as the other prisoners waited to board. Although the train was destined for the three mile long Mississippi River Island known as Rock Island, Illinois, it would take several days to arrive as a few hundred at a time poured into the camp. And by January 9th, 1864, just a few weeks after the Union victory at Missionary Ridge, all 6,158 captured Confederates had arrived.

The prison camp had already been notified to expect an influx of prisoners from the battle at

Missionary Ridge. On November 24, just one day before the battle, a guard assigned at the prison reported that he had "no blankets, no record book, no water in the prison yard, or clothing of any kind for the Confederates". And yet the prisoners were still boarded into the railcars and transported to what would become for many, their final destination.

Brown sat cramped in the middle of dozens of other soldiers piled almost on top of each other in the railcar. Although the conditions were not comfortable, the dozens of men cramped together generated enough body heat to help alleviate some of the bitter cold that seeped through the cracks in the railcar's door. And as the train traveled farther north crossing Indiana and much of Illinois, the train's lonely whistle faded into the sound of the howling wind as it slapped against the outside railcar's wall.

Brown's stomach churned and ached from lack of food, and he was becoming dehydrated. The cut above his left brow had finally ceased bleeding, but the stinging pain lingered as tiny pebbles of dirt and rock covered the open wound.

His mind drifted back to the battlefield. He remembered seeing the coattail of General Braxton Bragg at a distance as he narrowly escaped capture and certain death. The general's 5'10" slender frame faded into the background of his army's dead or captured men that now scattered the landscape. Brown remembered the general overseeing the camps in Tupelo, the headquarters of the Confederate Army of the West where he had spent the last several months before the day arrived when Bragg sent word to General Manigault that his brigade would be departing by train the following day for Chattanooga, Tennessee. He now longed to feel the warmth of his wife's touch, but his heart had known since the day he left Alabama that he might never see those comforts again, and Tupelo might become the only remaining semblance of home.

Hours turned into days as the train passed through depots heavily lined with young recruits waiting to replenish the Union army. The men's morale hit an all-time low as the reality of their demise became certain. The "Cause" was undoubtedly hopeless as they contemplated a war that never seemed to end.

The train's wheels squealed against the steel rails as it came to a halt near the prison camp. The heavy steel doors slid open exposing daylight and mounds of glittering white powder that reflected the sun's light against a backdrop of ice laden trees. The men's eyes were squinted as they emptied the boxcar falling into snow two feet deep.

Brown struggled to put one foot in front of the other as he started the fourth of a mile trek toward the prison camp. Of the four hundred plus men that arrived with him, dozens of them found themselves barefoot in knee deep snow and fighting temperatures unlike anything they had ever experienced in the South's steamy climate. It was a different kind of hell. A hell where freezing to death or suffering frostbite to the feet was a common occurrence. With no blankets or clothing for Confederate soldiers who were already thinly clad, there was little hope for survival.

Brown finally reached the barracks that typically held 120 men with three tiers of bunks. With the temperature registering just above freezing at 35 degrees Fahrenheit, Brown was shivering so violently that he could barely stand on two feet. He stumbled inside the building hardly equipped to house hundreds of soldiers. The roof was all that was separating the men from the night skies and the falling snow. There was no ceiling and little protection against the elements other than the walls that blocked the icy, cold wind gusts that swirled and howled outside.

Brown followed the line of men until he reached the bunk now designated for him. He fell against the bed and curled into a ball as dozens of his Confederate friends did the same. Within minutes, exhaustion overtook his body and his eyes closed.

By morning, Thomas Jefferson Brown joined the ranks of those who died within the walls of Rock Island, Illinois prison. Cause of death, exposure. His body lay motionless and hard as a block of ice. His fingers were unable to be pried open from the balled up fists that he held onto as his hands turned blue and slowly froze solid. The gash on his eye was no longer an open cut, but rather icy and sealed shut with traces of dried blood that had trickled down the side of his left cheek. Thomas Jefferson Brown would not suffer. His end had come fast, unlike many of the others who would spend months fighting disease and freezing temperatures.

Days later, Prater received word of his best friend's death making him the benefactor of Thomas Jefferson Brown's family, just as he had promised. While Brown's death was tragic, it was this destiny that was paving the way for a boy to be born four years later on April 21st, 1867 in Coosa County, Alabama. Because of his commitment to Thomas Jefferson Brown, Lewis Prater would father a child who would become a man destined to leave behind a legacy and a gift that only God could understand and the Devil could seek to destroy.

Chapter 3

The Gordon Hotel
January, 1880
Aberdeen, Mississippi

Seymour Prater stood outside the majestic red brick hotel located on East Commerce Street in Aberdeen, Mississippi. It had been years since Lewis Prater had married his best friend's widow and fathered a child with her. The couple lived a few years in Alabama after the War of the States ended and during Reconstruction. They then moved to Monroe

County, Mississippi where the roots of Seymour Prater's supernatural legacy would be planted.

The small southern town of Aberdeen was located on the banks of the Tombigbee River where explorer Hernando De Soto had once camped. It had survived the Civil War with most of its buildings still intact, and the town now boasted a population of over 2,300 people.

Seymour gazed up at the second floor of the hotel admiring its grandeur. It was the finest hotel along the Tombigbee River Banks in North Mississippi. And it served the area well since Aberdeen was one of Mississippi's busiest ports in the land where cotton was king.

He put one foot onto the front walkway leading into the hotel and stopped. He quickly leaned back just in time to avoid being hit in the face as the door swung open. Patrons of the hotel, one right after another, followed past the open door to the horses and buggies that lined the front outside entrance. Seymour watched as three then five men dressed in charcoal gray, pinstripe suits and matching top hats exited the hotel. As the last man stepped forward through the doorway, Seymour rushed inside letting the door swing back against him.

John Davenport, Captain of the Tombigbee River boat *Johnson*, stepped inside The Gordon Hotel for the first time since its opening day. The interior first floor was bustling with shoppers and patrons visiting the hotel for a haircut in the barbershop or for browsing in the various merchant shops where they might purchase a fine tailored gentlemen's suit or a handcrafted leather hat and matching shoes now affordable from their recent cotton trade. But Davenport's mood was heavy laden with doubt and anxiety as he mulled an uncertain future since preparing for his final voyage down the Tombigbee River. He had been enlisted to oversee the Hargrove's estate for the past few years transporting cotton when the river water levels allowed. Today, the riverboat was forced to dock overnight as the river's water level registered just below the ten feet depths that were considered safe for travel to Columbus, Mississippi. With overcast skies and heavy rain expected by nightfall, the trip would most likely become navigable by mid-morning.

Davenport lifted his hat and raked strands of hair away from his eyes. He pushed the hat back down fitting it against his head and stood still with one hand on his hip as he glanced around the giant open area of the first floor. His eyes circled the room as he admired the decorative grandeur. The hotel's front desk was lined with guests checking into the area's newest and finest lodging place along the upper Tombigbee River. Hundreds of passengers from the many Tombigbee Riverboats had already visited the hotel within weeks of its "Open for Business" announcement. The hotel had been made possible by investors with the promise of a prosperous future to its tenants. Among the many occupants were entrepreneurs such as grocers, clothing merchants, barbershops, and the local newspaper, The Aberdeen Weekly.

Davenport walked to a nearby sitting area decorated by fancy carved wooden chairs that were upholstered with plush, red velvet cushions. He sat down and examined his boots that were covered with dust from the nearby street. He was in the wrong place. The hotel and the likes of it were much too fancy for him and his blood. He was a riverboat captain who spent many of his years sleeping in a bunk hardly equipped to house his large, tall frame. He was used to uncomfortable conditions, and it was a life that he had become accustomed to. The scenic route along the flowing riverbanks was a pristine existence where raccoons played, deer roamed, and the occasional glimpse of a panther climbing a low lying tree branch caused a rapid heartbeat as it locked eyes with Davenport.

His heart was on the Tombigbee River, and the thought of this being his last trip for Mr. W. H. Hargrove caused him much grief since the railroad would now be the main means of transportation for Hargrove's cotton. Would his riverboat find more work possibly transporting other goods to the area or even as far south as Mobile?

***

The young Seymour Prater watched people come and go from a corner of the hotel lobby where he positioned himself away from the traffic and inquisitive eyes of the hotel staff. He was a quiet kid with a curious nature who rarely missed an opportunity to help someone or offer advice that seemed well beyond his youthful years. He had never understood his bizarre ability to "see" into the nature of others and even determine their destinies through mental pictures that played out in his mind. And he had never told anybody about his uncanny gift for fear of ridicule or disbelief. It was an oddity that he endured alone except when he "felt" the need to share an insight that could not be withheld within his good conscious.

Seymour watched through the storefront window as his mother shopped in one of the grocer markets inside the hotel. Martha Prater savored the smell of fresh bread as she quickly lifted it to her nose before placing it into her basket. She joined dozens of other women this morning eager to shop among the hotel's many venues, and she had allowed Seymour to accompany her to the hotel since she would most likely need his assistance to carry her bags.

An invisible prompt suddenly caused Seymour to look away and turn his eyes toward John Davenport sitting in a chair across the room. He studied the man's expression and the way his body leaned forward in the chair, not sitting all the way back. He watched as the man studied his own feet. He noticed him bend over and down as he wiped his first two fingers across the toe of his boot before examining the rug beneath his feet.

Seymour's uncanny gift of insight began to come alive at that moment as he received invisible messages of the man's thoughts. It was as if he was plugging into a radio frequency that only John Davenport could hear, yet Seymour was an unknown invader who, regardless of his harmless intent, could no more control his own inclinations to see into the lives of another than he could control his body's natural urges of hunger or excretion.

Davenport's anxiety was real. He thought about the possibility of the railroad now taking over as a main means of transport. He knew that his security had been threatened. And while Davenport's thoughts filled the rafters of his mind, Seymour Prater listened in as the static became clearer. What would he do with the last two decades of his life now gone? He was a river captain, and John Davenport could not conceive of any other identity.

"I saw you on the riverboat *Johnson.* You work for Mr. Hargrove, but you're scared that you won't have a job in a few months when he starts using the railroad. Don't worry." Seymour paused as Davenport stared in disbelief.

"Who are you, Kid? How do you know this?" Davenport leaned back in his seat and took a deep breath.

"I'm nobody, Sir. I just have some sort of odd talent, I guess." Seymour looked away and studied his hands folded in his lap.

"What do you mean that you 'saw me on the riverboat Johnson'?" Davenport was quickly forming an opinion about the boy, but he had questions of his own to ask.

"Oh, I just meant that I saw you in my mind. That's all." Seymour rubbed his fingers across his brow.

"You saw me in your mind? Can you see other things?" Davenport was now intrigued. He was well aware of Seymour's rare natural talent. He had only known one other person in his lifetime with the 'gift', but the former slave girl who lived on the Hargrove Plantation had been dead for years. Before being stricken with Typhoid Fever, she was considered to be Hargrove's most prized possession and often advised Master Hargrove of unseen troubles on the horizon. He had witnessed the supernatural wonders of her insights many times, and she had confided her secrets in Hargrove and Davenport who was often by his side more than anyone else in his circle. Davenport knew how she kept her abilities sharp. He knew what she was doing each morning before sunrise when she left the cabin and walked twenty feet to the old tree stump overshadowed by hanging vine and honeysuckle blooms. He had seen her sitting there with her eyes closed, not saying a word. Just still and quiet for several minutes until it was time to return to the morning's work at the plantation mansion.

"Yes, Sir. I see pictures. Not all the time, but I started seeing pictures about you almost as soon as you entered the hotel. And I knew that I should tell you not to worry." Seymour spoke barely above a whisper as people passed near them on their way to the hotel's front check-in counter.

Davenport sighed with relief and lifted his hat as he combed his hair back once again before standing to leave the hotel. He looked at the youth now standing before him in the hotel lobby. Seymour Prater had given him an important and timely message. He had offered encouragement and hope. And now Davenport knew that he must instruct Seymour Prater about the reality of his visions. He must instruct him to develop his abilities.

"What's your name, Kid?" Davenport reached out and patted Seymour on the shoulder.

"Seymour. Seymour Prater, Sir."

"Well, my good man, Seymour, it wasn't an accident that our paths crossed today. You understand that, don't you?" Davenport looked hard and straight in Seymour's eyes.

"Yes, Sir. I believe so."

"Good. Then here's what you need to do from this day forward and for the rest of your life. You must develop this special gift that you have. It will be your calling in life. You understand?"

Seymour nodded. "Yes, but I don't know how."

Davenport motioned for Seymour to step aside as hotel guests began to take the now empty seats that they had vacated. They took a few steps forward and stopped near the hotel's front door.

Davenport spoke clearly. "You must learn how to clear your mind and focus, Young Man. It's called meditation. You must practice this every day for a few minutes. It will open channels to you. First, find a quiet place to be alone and focus on a question in your mind, then be quiet and wait."

Seymour nodded in spite of the slight bit of confusion that he was feeling. He repeated Davenport's instructions. "Focus and clear my mind."

"Yes, that's right. I've only known one other person who could do it. And you will get better at it as time goes by. Now I have to get going. You do what I told you." Davenport patted Seymour once again on the back and reached for the door handle.

Seymour stood still in the doorway as he paused and watched John Davenport walk out ahead of him. Davenport looked back over his shoulder one last time and nodded as he spoke. "Focus. Good luck, young man." He turned the corner at the north end of the hotel and faded out of sight.

It would be the first and last time that Seymour ever saw John Davenport, but this chance meeting and Davenport's instructions would prove to be the most important guidance that he would ever receive. Davenport's timely message had set the stage for the beginning of what would become a supernatural legacy destined to be delivered by none other than Seymour R. Prater.

Chapter 4

January 3, 1931.
Deep in the Mississippi Delta of Carrollton,
Mississippi.
10:50 p.m.

Arthur Floyd reached inside the glass candy dish and grabbed a round piece of Peppermint candy. He placed the silver lid back on the jar as the metal tapped against the glass and clinked shut. A flicker of light entered his peripheral vision as it danced up and down the wall beside him. He turned and looked down the aisle toward the front door of the country store that he had owned and operated for the past ten years. A light bulb hung from an electrical cable near the front door of the store, but it was now swinging back and forth as if someone had pushed it. He studied the fixture and glanced around the displays of flour sacks and wooden crates located beneath the light. No one was visible to his eyes, but his ears weren't capable of alerting him of any danger since he had been born deaf and had spent all of his life in a world of silence.

Mr. Floyd mumbled thoughts of confusion and anxiety as he started toward the front of the room. His eyes were wide as he scanned the aisles from right to left, looking for the source that caused the swinging light fixture. He moved slowly toward the front door, his eyes now fixed on the lock that he had intended to secure. He wasn't aware of the occasional pop that his joints were making as he slowly walked forward. At 56 years old, Arthur Floyd suffered from chronic arthritis in his legs and hips. Although he was of average height at 5'9" and average weight of 159 pounds, he moved with a speed about the same as a turtle.

Arthur stopped and stood under the light fixture. Something didn't feel right. The front door was closed, and it appeared that he was the only person in the store. Yet someone sat crouched near the endcap where Arthur Floyd stood. Watching and waiting for just the right moment. The whites of his eyes were laced with a trail of bloody veins in the background of the deep, dark brown iris that matched the color of his skin.

The intruder grasped the handle of the ax tighter until the skin on his knuckles paled in color. He listened to Arthur's footsteps on the wide wood plank floor and the crackling and popping of Arthur's joints. He was just seconds away from the ambush that he and his brother were now about to execute.

Arthur paused and reached over his head to grab the swinging light. Just as his hand closed around the cable and the swinging ceased, the blunt force of an ax landed in the back of Arthur Floyd's head, not once, but twice. Powerful and fast.

One last guttural sound escaped from his lips as his hand dropped from the cable and his body collapsed to the floor with a hard and loud thud. Blood splatters covered the flour sacks and the front glass window while a pool of the bright crimson life force formed around his face branching off into small canals that oozed from the source of its flow. Arthur Floyd's demise was an immediate death with no warning other than the swinging light fixture that had alerted him of someone's presence.

The intruder rushed to Arthur's side and reached in his left side pants pocket digging for the keys to the store's office where Arthur kept operating cash and customer account records. He jerked out a large wad of keys attached to a metal ring then stood and reached for the front door as his brother turned the doorknob and pushed the front door open. He entered the store and stepped around Arthur Floyd's body. The murderer who had delivered the fatal blows reached for the lock and secured the door.

"You got the keys?" He whispered aloud.

The killer nodded and motioned for his brother to follow as he raced toward the back of the store and the office area. He quickly tried several keys before finding a match then pushed the door open and without wasting a fraction of a second, the two brothers emptied the safe, Arthur's desk, and the nearby book casings of any valuables that might be useful.

The murderer hurriedly walked to the corner of the door and glanced out into the store one last time before making his escape. His eyes focused on the dead man's body lying face down in the middle of the aisle near the front of the store, his left arm bent backwards and his palm closed still clutching the round piece of peppermint candy that he had pulled from the candy jar just moments before.

As the killer turned to walk out the back door, he remembered the weapon and ran to retrieve the ax now lying beside the corpse's head. He reached down and grabbed the handle clutching it as tightly as he had when he delivered the fatal blow that killed Arthur

Floyd. As he stood back up, the killer's head tapped the lightbulb hanging from the cable. Startled by the touch and his fear of being caught inside the store with the dead body, the killer gasped and dropped the murder weapon onto the floor. He then made a fast retreat to the backdoor exit. As the door slammed behind him, a deafening silence filled the room with only the sound of the swinging electrical cable and its metal chain clinking against the lightbulb.

Swinging back and forth. Back and forth.

Clink. Clink. Clink.

A deaf man lay dead at the hands of two brothers who he had known. They had owed Arthur money. Money for goods that his generosity had allowed them. As Arthur Floyd lay dead, his eyelids were fixed and wide open with a stare that could only predict the haunting to come and a dead man's desire for revenge.

At just before dawn the following morning, the killer awakened, grabbed his coat off the back of a chair, and hurried out the door. He must return to the scene of the crime one final time. He had left the murder weapon and keys lying in the floor, but he had to get rid of it. He couldn't allow himself to get spooked again. He would do it fast. If he got there before the sun came up, he could get rid of it, and he knew where he could hide it. In the cistern at the bottom of the stairs leading to the basement. He had been down there once when he had helped Arthur Floyd carry some tools for storage. It was the perfect hiding place. The cistern in the basement stayed dry most of the time, and the killer reasoned that no one really knew that it was there since it wasn't being used anymore.

He hurried down the path that led to the Walton Farm. As he neared the rear entrance to Arthur's store, he could see the hanging light bulb that still illuminated the front of the store. He stepped onto the back porch steps and climbed to the top. The back door was still slightly ajar.

His breathing became heavy as he neared the opening to the store. The fear of being caught began to creep over him once again as he pushed the door open and rushed up the center aisle where the dead body of Arthur Floyd lay decaying. With wide eyes, the killer looked straight ahead at the front windows where blood had splattered across the glass. He then glanced down at the floor and searched for the ax and keys that he had dropped a few hours before. His eyes quickly landed on the murder weapon lying next to Arthur's right hand. The killer reached down, grabbed the keys and ax, and ran toward Arthur's office where the door leading to the basement was located.

He flung the door open and searched for a light, running his hand along the right side of the wall. His fingers found the wall socket and switched it to on as he skipped two steps at a time down the basement stairs. He reached the bottom of the stairs and swiftly walked to the cistern where he uncapped the covered hole by removing the wood board that had sealed it shut.

He pushed the board aside creating an opening and tossed the keys and ax to the bottom. The ax tapped the side of the metal receptacle and echoed as it hit a tiny puddle of water settled on the cistern's floor. The killer then pushed the wood cover back in place and raced back up the stairs, flicking off the light, and slamming the door behind him.

As he sprinted across the floor toward the exit, his eyes caught a glimpse of a shadow lurking up the wall beside him. Its form took the shape of a human body as it moved away from the wall. The killer jerked around. His pale blue eyes were bloodshot and watery as he stared at a strange black shadow that seemed to be suspended in air near the center aisle of the store. And then it vanished right before his eyes. Just as quickly as it had entered his peripheral vision, it was gone.

A freezing chill swept over the guilty man's body as he backed one foot at a time away from the center aisle and out the back door. With a sudden and uncanny awareness, the killer sensed the magnitude of his sin and the consequences that were coming.

Chapter 5

Monday morning, January 5, 1931

At just past sunrise, Phoebe Jones made her way along the familiar path to Arthur Floyd's store, limping on her bad foot from time to time. Although years had passed since the accident when she was trampled by a horse gone wild, she still had pain from where the bones in her foot had been shattered and had not grown back correctly.

The morning sun was bright and warming, but the cold January air still chilled her arms in spite of the wool wrap that covered her. Dust covered her shoes as she walked the dirt path located just beyond the wood shack she called home. As she neared the edge of the trees, she noticed the light bulb dangling from its cord, illuminating the inside of the store now just a few steps away.

Phoebe walked around the side of the building toward the front porch. She stepped onto the bottom wood step and began to climb the stairs when she noticed blood splatters covering the front window. Her face screwed up into a frightened stare as she inched closer toward the front door. She slowly walked to the window and leaned forward. She peered in and looked up and down the aisles. Then she let her eyes shift to both sides of the door. Nothing. But in a split second as she lowered her gaze to the floor, her body froze and her eyes became fixed on the sight before her. The dead and decaying corpse of Arthur Floyd was still lying face down in the same position where he had fallen two nights before. The gaping hole in his head was clearly visible, exposing brain matter in the busted, split skull.

Phoebe gasped as her hand immediately covered her mouth and tears spilled over her eyelids. She mouthed words of horror, shaking her head back and forth and slowly moving away from the door. Her feet were clumsy causing her to stumble off the porch and down the stairs, but she managed to regain her footing. Without looking back, she made a swift dash toward the sheriff's office at the end of the street.

Sheriff Frank Baker, a short and stocky man in his late 40's, sat in a wood swivel chair with his legs propped up on the corner of the desk as he read The Conservative. Although the newspaper's headquarters was located in the city of Winona about ten miles away, The Conservative covered the Carrollton area and any news events that happened there. It was Carrollton's link to the surrounding counties in Mississippi. If it happened in Carrollton, it was up to The Conservative to report it. Otherwise, no one would ever know.

Sheriff Baker heard screams coming from outside the office door. He jerked his legs down off the desk and looked out the front window where he saw Phoebe running straight toward his office, her eyes filled with tears and a terrifying fright that he had never seen in her before today. He rushed around his desk and flung the door open.

"What? What is it, Ms. Phoebe?" The sheriff asked in a southern drawl heard only in the deepest recesses of the American South.

"It's Mr. Floyd. He's dead. There's blood everywhere, Sheriff. Blood everywhere, I tell you!" Phoebe gasped, her breath forming a cold fog with each word that escaped her lips. She wiped an invisible sweat from her face that she imagined to be there, but her cheeks were only moistened by the tears that had seeped from her eyelids as she became the first witness of Arthur Floyd's murdered body.

The sheriff grabbed his hat off the corner of his desk and placed it on his head as he slammed the door behind him and motioned for Phoebe to follow him back to the store. He raced up the front steps and reached for the door handle. He turned the knob and pushed the door to no avail. It was still locked. He leaned forward and peered through the front window. Blood puddles still pooled around Arthur Floyd's head due to the cold January temperatures that delayed the decaying process and helped preserve the crime scene. With temperatures near freezing, rigor mortis and the putrefaction of tissues had been slowed.

The sheriff turned and started down the steps then turned back to face Phoebe who was reluctant to go any further toward the front door. He noticed the morbid stare in her eyes.

"Phoebe, go fetch Deputy Phillips, and tell him we have a body." Sheriff Baker's tone was somber. He paused as Phoebe stared back.

"Go. I'll get in the store somehow." The sheriff jumped off the top step to the ground and began to walk toward the back of the store.

"Yes Sir." Phoebe struggled to ease her trembling hands as she rubbed them together. She then rushed past the sheriff and onto the same path that had brought her here.

Deputy Phillips lived about a ten minute walk away from the town's main street. He was the sheriff's right hand man and the town's local funeral director. It would be up to Phillips to transport the body of Arthur Floyd, deliver the news to Arthur's family, and arrange the burial after the investigation.

As Phoebe found herself at the deputy's house, she hurried across the front yard, climbed the two porch steps, and rapped on the screen door.

"Mr. Phillips! Mr. Phillips! The sheriff needs you!" Phoebe shouted with urgency.

A brief moment passed before the deputy appeared. Before he could ask any questions, Phoebe informed him of the morning's event.

"Mr. Floyd is dead. He's dead in his store. You've got to come now." The reality of her words sank in deep as Phoebe wrapped the cotton shawl tighter against her arms.

Deputy Phillips grabbed a coat and hat from the wall leaving his wife still sleeping in the comforts of their bed. He and his bride had been married twenty years, and she rarely missed a day of preparing breakfast for the deputy, but this morning, he quietly walked out the door and followed Phoebe across the front yard. As they both neared the path, he began asking questions.

"Where is the sheriff now?"

"He's at the store. He can't get in the front door. It's locked. He's gonna try to get in the back, but he told me to come get you." Phoebe explained.

"I see. Wait just a minute." He turned around and ran back toward the house with Phoebe following close behind. As he flung open the door, he grabbed a set of keys hanging on the inside wall.

"Come on. Get in on the other side." The deputy noticed the fear that consumed Phoebe as her hands trembled while reaching for the door handle.

Phoebe climbed inside the town coroner's car and chewed her fingernails. She hoped that she could get back to the Walton Farm where she was the family's main housekeeper and cook. Her morning trip was only meant to purchase flour and a few other staples necessary for baking, and if she didn't return soon, the Walton's would be looking for her.

Deputy Phillips turned onto Main Street and drove the car to the front of the store. He stopped and pushed the gear shift into park as he reached for the door handle and turned the key in the car's ignition to off. He leaned over the back of the seat and grabbed a small black trunk that contained a camera and a few other items he would need at the scene. He then quickly pushed the door open and got out as he surveyed the area.

The deputy saw the sheriff standing inside the store and headed for the steps. Sheriff Baker motioned for him to stop. He lifted his hat off his head and placed it on top of a rack of canned goods. The sheriff then ran his fingers across his thin, graying hair and released a heavy sigh. He raised his arm and motioned with his thumb over his shoulder.

"Go around to the back. There's blood all over the place on the other side of that door!" The sheriff's voice was loud and clear.

Deputy Phillips turned; his 6'2" frame enabled him to take long strides as he rushed to the back of the brick building and jumped onto the back porch. He darted through the door and up the aisle to join the sheriff now standing over Arthur Floyd's corpse.

Although the cold temperature inside the store had delayed the decaying process, it was apparent to Phillips that the body had been dead for more than 24 hours. The town coroner slowly bent down resting his knees on the floor while sitting against his ankles as he examined the gaping wound on the back of Arthur Floyd's skull. He pulled a tape measure from his pocket and held it over the victim's head without touching the body. He noticed the purple-red skin discoloration on Arthur's face, neck, and hands. And Arthur's eyes remained open and fixed with the eyelids frozen in place.

The fatal injury measured approximately four inches along the middle left area of the skull. Phillips analyzed the slit and determined that the weapon was administered with a blunt force so powerful that it left broken bits of the victim's cranium within the gray and black hair now stained with dry blood. Phillips stood up and removed a camera from the trunk that he had set next to the center aisle. He began snapping pictures while the sheriff recorded details of the scene on a small notepad he carried in his shirt pocket.

"Who could do this to Arthur?" Deputy Phillips asked as he moved around the body photographing the scene at different angles. "Somebody wanted him dead quick. Whoever did this hit him more than once. You see any weapons lying around?"

The sheriff shook his head. "Nothing, but look at his left hand. There's a piece of candy folded inside his hand. Looks like he was caught by surprise. Somebody was waiting for him right here."

A distant memory suddenly flashed through the sheriff's mind. He remembered the last dead body that he had looked upon, and he remembered the displeasure of having to notify the next of kin. It was a part of the job that he disliked the most, but a fifteen year career in law enforcement had made Baker a thankful man for the devoted woman and son he had at home. He believed in living by the law and executing the proper punishments for those who broke the law, but he was a kind man behind the tough exterior and rugged ways. For those who had known Baker all his life, he was just a stern man with a deep, harsh voice that softened like butter in the presence of his wife.

The deputy looked at Baker with raised eyebrows. "A robbery?" He scratched his brow and wiped his nose with a handkerchief he pulled from his back pants pocket.

"Yeah, looks like they went through Arthur's desk." The sheriff shook his head as he looked down at Mr. Floyd's dead body. The whole town would be affected by the killing.   Everyone was a neighbor to each other in this small community known as Carrollton.   The Mississippi Delta town was located on the south side of Big Sand Creek with a population of approximately five hundred twenty people.   Half of those people were black and the other half white. Most everyone got along well with little or no crime to speak of until now.

The deputy looked at the sheriff and pointed toward Phoebe who stood at the backdoor of the store. "What does she know?"

The sheriff shook his head.   "Don't know yet. She came running to my office just a few minutes ago. She found the body."

"But she didn't enter the store, did she?" The deputy asked.

"Not that I know of."   The sheriff looked at Phoebe who refused to step any further than the back door entrance.

"Ms. Phoebe?"   The deputy called out.

Phoebe peered around a display case blocking her view of the deputy. "Yes, Sir?"

"I need you to stay right there for a few minutes. I'm gonna need to ask you a few questions." The deputy watched her.

Phoebe nodded then objected. "Yes, Sir, but Mrs. Walton gonna come looking for me in a minute, Sir."

The sheriff looked at Phillips and nodded indicating that he would take care of Phoebe while the deputy prepared to remove the body.

The sheriff walked to the back of the store and faced Phoebe. "Ms. Phoebe, were you the only one here when you found Mr. Floyd?"

"Yes, Sir." Phoebe's eyes watered.

"Where were you when you found him?"

"I was standing on the front porch, Sir. I saw him through the front door."

"What did you do next?" The sheriff studied her.

"I started crying and ran to get you!" Phoebe's eyes moistened again.

"And you didn't see anybody else around here? Nobody walking past the store or anything else going on?"

Phoebe shook her head with her eyes closed and her face screwed up in a grievous expression.

The sheriff nodded and took a deep breath. "Ok, you can go on home now."

Phoebe backed out the door without turning around. Images of Arthur Floyd's face left an imprint in her mind as she struggled to erase the memory, but it haunted her. They were horrific images that warned her of the coming resurrection of a murdered man. She had looked into the eyes of Arthur Floyd. A dead man with a soul now doomed to be a wandering ghost, and although she had not touched the corpse or any of his belongings, she felt unclean.

Yes, she must get back to the Walton Farm and her home as soon as possible. She had to tell everyone who would listen. Arthur Floyd had been murdered in cold blood, and his ghost would surely seek revenge upon the town of Carrollton, Mississippi.

End of sample

L. Sydney Fisher

"I first witnessed the paranormal at the tender age of eight. This experience unlocked a doorway to a world full of unexplained mysteries, miraculous insights, and terrifying ghostly visits that have spanned a lifetime. Join me as I explore these stories...one book at a time." ~L. Sydney Fisher

Sydney on the WEB:
Http://www.LSydneyFisher.com

www.ingramcontent.com/pod-product-compliance
Lightning Source LLC
Chambersburg PA
CBHW060011050426
42448CB00012B/2705